EDUCATION AND THE GOOD LIFE

EDUCATION
AND THE
GOOD LIFE

BERTRAND RUSSELL

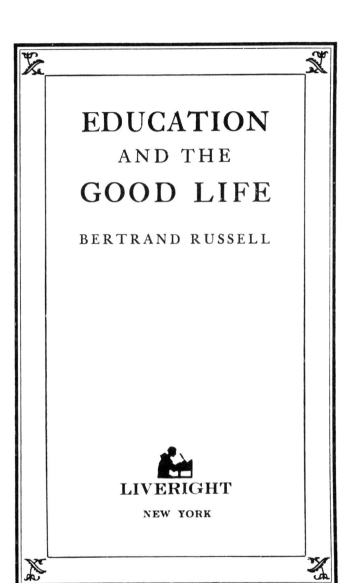

LIVERIGHT
NEW YORK

LIVERIGHT PAPERBOUND EDITION   1970

CONTENTS

PART III

INTELLECTUAL EDUCATION

INTRODUCTION

THERE must be in the world many parents who, like the present author, have young children whom they are anxious to educate as well as possible, but reluctant to expose to the evils of most existing educational institutions. The difficulties of such parents are not soluble by any effort on the part of isolated individuals. It is of course possible to bring up children at home by means of governesses and tutors, but this plan deprives them of the companionship which their nature craves, and without which some essential elements of education must be lacking. Moreover it is extremely bad for a boy or girl to be made to feel "odd" and different from other boys and girls: this feeling, when traced to parents as its cause, is almost certain to rouse resentment against them, leading to a love of all that they most dislike. The conscientious parent may be driven by these considerations to send his boys and girls to schools in which he sees grave defects, merely because no existing schools seem to him satisfactory—or, if any are satisfactory, they are not in his neighbourhood. Thus the cause of educational reform is forced upon conscientious parents, not only for the good of the community, but also for the good of their own children. If the parents are well-to-do, it is not necessary to the solution of their private problem that *all* schools should be good, but only that there should be some good school geographically available. But for wage-earning parents nothing suffices except reform in the elementary schools. As one parent will object to the reforms which another parent desires, nothing will serve except an energetic educational propaganda, which is not likely to prove effective until long after the reformer's children are grown up. Thus from love for our own children we are driven, step by step, into the wider sphere of politics and philosophy.

From this wider sphere I desire, in the following pages, to remain aloof as far as possible. The greater part of what I have to say will not be dependent upon the views that I may happen to hold as regards the major controversies of our age. But *complete* independence in this regard is impossible. The education we desire for our children must depend upon our ideals of human character, and our hopes as to the part they are to play in the community. A pacifist will not desire for his children the education which seems good to a militarist; the educational outlook of a communist will not be

the same as that of an individualist. To come
to a more fundamental cleavage: there can be
no agreement between those who regard education as a means of instilling certain definite beliefs and those who think that it should produce
the power of independent judgment. Where
such issues are relevant, it would be idle to
shirk them. At the same time, there is a considerable body of new knowledge in psychology
and pedagogy which is independent of these
ultimate questions, and has an intimate bearing
on education. Already it has produced very
important results, but a great deal remains to
be done before its teachings have been fully
assimilated. This is especially true of the first
five years of life; these have been found to have
an importance far greater than that formerly
attributed to them, which involves a corre-
sponding increase in the educational importance of parents. My aim and purpose, wherever possible, will be to avoid controversial
issues. Polemical writing is necessary in some
spheres; but in addressing parents one may
assume a sincere desire for the welfare of their
offspring, and this alone, in conjunction with
modern knowledge, suffices to decide a very
large number of educational problems. What
I have to say is the outcome of perplexities in
regard to my own children; it is therefore not
remote or theoretical, and may, I hope, help to

clarify the thoughts of other parents faced with a like perplexity, whether in the way of agreement with my conclusions or the opposite. The opinions of parents are immensely important, because, for lack of expert knowledge, parents are too often a drag upon the best educationists. If parents desire a good education for their children, there will, I am convinced, be no lack of teachers willing and able to give it.

I propose, in what follows, to consider first the aims of education: the kind of individuals, and the kind of community, that we may reasonably hope to see produced by education applied to raw material of the present quality. I ignore the question of the improvement of the breed, whether by eugenics or by any other process, natural or artificial, since this is essentially outside the problems of education. But I attach great weight to modern psychological discoveries which tend to show that character is determined by early education to a much greater extent than was thought by the most enthusiastic educationists of former generations. I distinguish between education of character and education in knowledge, which may be called instruction in the strict sense. The distinction is useful, though not ultimate: some virtues are required in a pupil who is to become instructed, and much knowledge is required for

the successful practice of many important virtues. For purposes of discussion, however,
instruction can be kept apart from education
of character. I shall deal first with education
of character, because it is especially important
in early years; but I shall carry it through to
adolescence, and deal, under this head, with
the important question of sex education.
Finally, I shall discuss intellectual education,
its aims, its curriculum, and its possibilities,
from the first lessons in reading and writing
to the end of the university years. The further
education which men and women derive from
life and the world I shall regard as lying outside my scope; but to make men and women
capable of learning from experience should be
one of the aims which early education should
keep most prominently in view.

.

PART I
EDUCATION AND THE GOOD LIFE

EDUCATION AND THE
GOOD LIFE

CHAPTER I

POSTULATES OF MODERN EDUCATIONAL THEORY

IN reading even the best treatises on education written in former times, one becomes aware of certain changes that have come over educational theory. The two great reformers of educational theory before the nineteenth century were Locke and Rousseau. Both deserved their reputation, for both repudiated many errors which were widespread when they wrote. But neither went as far in his own direction as almost all modern educationists go. Both, for example, belong to the tendency which led to liberalism and democracy; yet both consider only the education of an aristocratic boy, to which one man's whole time is devoted. However excellent might be the results of such a system, no man with a modern outlook would give it serious consideration, because it is arithmetically impossible for every child to absorb the whole time of an adult tutor. The system is therefore one which can only be employed by a privileged caste; in a just world, its existence would be impossible. The modern man, though he may seek special advantages for his own children in practice, does not consider the theoretical problem solved except by some method of education which could be open to all, or at least to all whose capacities render them capable of profiting by it. I do not mean that the well-to-do should, here and now, forego educational opportunities which, in the existing world, are not open to all. To do that would be to sacrifice civilization to justice. What I do mean is that the educational system we must aim at producing in the future is one which gives to every boy and girl an opportunity for the best that exists. The ideal system of education must be democratic, although that ideal is not immediately attainable. This, I think, would, nowadays, be pretty generally conceded. In this sense, I shall keep democracy in view. Whatever I shall advocate will be capable of being universal, though the individual should not meantime sacrifice his children to the badness of what is common, if he has the intelligence and the opportunity to secure something better. Even this very attentuated form of democratic principle is absent from the treatises of Locke and Rousseau. Although the latter was a disbeliever in aristocracy, he never perceived the implications of his disbelief where education was concerned.

This matter of democracy and education is one as to which clarity is important. It would be disastrous to insist upon a dead level of uniformity. Some boys and girls are cleverer than others, and can derive more benefit from higher education. Some teachers have been better trained or have more native aptitude than others, but it is impossible that everybody should be taught by the few best teachers. Even if the highest education were desirable for all, which I doubt, it is impossible that all should have it at present, and therefore a crude application of democratic principles might lead to the conclusion that none should have it. Such a view, if adopted, would be fatal to scientific progress, and would make the general level of education a hundred years hence needlessly low. Progress should not be sacrificed to a mechanical equality at the present moment; we must approach educational democracy carefully, so as to destroy in the process as little as possible of the valuable products that happen to have been associated with social injustice.

But we cannot regard a method of education as satisfactory if it is one which could not possibly be universal. The children of rich people often have, in addition to their mother, a nurse, a nurserymaid, and a share in the other domestic servants; this involves an amount of attention which could never, in any social system, be given to all children. It is very doubtful whether carefully tended children really gain by being made unnecessarily parasitic, but in any case no impartial person can recommend special advantages for the few, except for special reasons, such as feeble-mindedness or genius. The wise parent, at the present day, is likely to choose, if he can, some method of education for his children which is not in fact universal, and for the sake of experiment it is desirable that parents should have the opportunity of trying new methods. But they ought to be such as could be made universal, if found to produce good results, not such as must from their very nature be confined to a privileged few. Fortunately, some of the best elements in modern educational theory and practice have had an extremely democratic origin; for example, Madame Montessori's work began with nursery schools in slums. In higher education, exceptional opportunity for exceptional ability is indispensable, but otherwise there is no reason why any child should suffer from the adoption of systems which might be adopted by all.

There is another modern tendency in education, which is connected with democracy, but perhaps somewhat more open to question—I mean the tendency to make education useful rather than ornamental. The connection of the ornamental with aristocracy has been set forth searchingly in Veblen's "Theory of the Leisure Class", but it is only the educational aspect of this connection that concerns us. In male education, the matter is bound up with the controversy between a classical and a "modern" education; in the education of girls, it is part of the conflict between the ideal of the "gentlewoman" and the desire to train girls to be self-supporting. But the whole educational problem, where women are concerned, has been distorted by the desire for sex equality: there has been an attempt to acquire the same education as that given to boys, even where it was by no means good in itself. Consequently women educators have aimed at giving to their girls such "useless" knowledge as is given to boys of the same class, and have been bitter opponents of the notion that some part of female education should be a technical training for motherhood. These cross-currents make the tendency that I am considering in some respects less definite where women are concerned, though the decay of the ideal of the "fine lady" is one of the most noteworthy examples of the tendency. In order to avoid confusing the issue, I shall for the moment confine myself to male education.

Many separate controversies, in all of which other questions arise, are in part dependent upon our present question. Should boys learn mainly classics or mainly science? Among other considerations, one is that the classics are ornamental and science is useful. Should education as soon as possible become technical instruction for some trade or profession? Again the controversy between the useful and the ornamental is relevant, though not decisive. Should children be taught to enunciate correctly and to have pleasant manners, or are these mere relics of aristocracy? Is appreciation of art a thing of any value except in the artist? Should spelling be phonetic? All these and many other controversies are argued in part in terms of the controversy between the useful and the ornamental.

Nevertheless, I believe the whole controversy to be unreal. As soon as the terms are defined, it melts away. If we interpret "useful" broadly and "ornamental" narrowly, the one side has it; in the contrary interpretation, the other side has it. In the widest and most correct sense of the word, an activity is "useful" when it has good results. And these results must be "good" in some other sense than merely "useful", or else we have no true definition.

We cannot say that a useful activity is one which has useful results. The essence of what is "useful" is that it ministers to some result which is not merely useful. Sometimes a long chain of results is necessary before the final result is reached which can be called simply "good". A plough is useful because it breaks up the ground. But breaking up the ground is not good on its own account: it is in turn merely useful because it enables seed to be sown. This is useful because it produces grain, which is useful because it produces bread, which is useful because it preserves life. But life must be capable of some intrinsic value: if life were merely useful as a means to other life, it would not be useful at all. Life may be good or bad according to circumstances; it may therefore also be useful, when it is a means to good life. Somewhere we must get beyond the chain of successive utilities, and find a peg from which the chain is to hang; if not, there is no real usefulness in any link of the chain. When "useful" is defined in this way, there can be no question whether education should be useful. Of course it should, since the process of educating is a means to an end, not an end in itself. But that is not quite what the advocates of utility in education have in mind. What they are urging is that the *result* of education should be useful: put crudely, they would say that an educated man is a man who knows how to make machines. If we ask what is the use of machines, the answer is ultimately that they produce necessaries and comforts for the body —food, clothing, houses, etc. Thus we find that the advocate of utility, in the sense in which his view is questionable, is a man who attaches intrinsic value only to physical satisfactions: the "useful", for him, is that which helps us to gratify the needs and desires of the body. When this is what is really meant, the advocate of utility is certainly in the wrong if he is enunciating an ultimate philosophy, though in a world where many people are starving he may be right as a politician, since the satisfaction of physical needs may be at the moment more urgent than anything else.

Much the same sort of dissection is necessary in considering the other side of this controversy. To call the other side "ornamental" is, of course, to concede a point to the advocate of utility, since "ornament" is understood to be more or less trivial. The epithet "ornamental" is quite justified as applied to the traditional conception of a "gentleman" or a "lady". The eighteenth-century gentleman spoke with a refined accent, quoted the classics on appropriate occasions, dressed in the fashion, understood punctilio and knew when a duel

would advance his reputation. There is a man
in "The Rape of the Lock" who was

> of amber snuff-box justly vain,
> And the nice conduct of a clouded cane.

His education had been ornamental in the nar-
rowest sense, and in our age few of us are rich
enough to be content with his accomplishments.
The ideal of an "ornamental" education in the
old sense is aristocratic: it presupposes a class
with plenty of money and no need to work.
Fine gentlemen and fine ladies are charming
to contemplate in history; their memoirs and
their country houses give us a certain kind of
pleasure which we no longer provide for our
posterity. But their excellences, even when
real, were by no means supreme, and they were
an incredibly expensive product: Hogarth's
"Gin Lane" gives a vivid idea of the price that
was paid for them. No one nowadays would
advocate an ornamental education in this narrow sense.

But that is not the real issue. The real issue
is: should we, in education, aim at filling the
mind with knowledge which has direct practical utility, or should we try to give our pupils
mental possessions which are good on their own
account? It is useful to know that there are
twelve inches in a foot, and three feet in a
yard, but this knowledge has no intrinsic value;

to those who live where the metric system is in
use, it is utterly worthless.   To appreciate
"Hamlet", on the other hand, will not be much
use in practical life, except in those rare cases
where a man is called upon to kill his uncle;
but it gives a man a mental possession which he
would be sorry to be without, and makes him
in some sense a more excellent human being.
It is this latter sort of knowledge that is preferred by the man who argues that utility is
not the sole aim of education.

There appear to be three different substan-
tial issues wrapped up in the debate between
advocates of a utilitarian education and their
opponents.   There is first a form of the debate
between aristocrats and democrats, the former
holding that the privileged class should be
taught to employ its leisure in ways that are
agreeable to itself, while the subordinate class
should be taught to employ its labour in ways
that are useful to others.   The opposition of the
democrats to this view tends to be somewhat
confused: they dislike the teaching of what is
useless to the aristocrat, and at the same time
argue that the wage-earner's education should
not be confined to what is useful.   Thus we find
a democratic opposition to the old-fashioned
classical education in the public schools, combined with a democratic demand that working
men should have opportunities for learning

Latin and Greek. This attitude, even though it may imply some lack of theoretical clarity, is on the whole right in practice. The democrat does not wish to divide the community into two sections, one useful and one ornamental; he will therefore give more merely useful knowledge to the hitherto merely ornamental classes, and more merely delightful knowledge to the hitherto merely useful classes. But democracy, *per se*, does not decide the proportions in which these ingredients should be mixed.

The second issue is between men who aim only at material goods and men who care for mental delights. Most modern well-to-do Englishmen and Americans, if they were transported by magic into the age of Elizabeth, would wish themselves back in the modern world. The society of Shakespeare and Raleigh and Sir Philip Sydney, the exquisite music, the beauty of the architecture would not console them for the absence of bath-rooms, tea and coffee, motor-cars, and other material comforts of which that age was ignorant. Such men, except in so far as they are influenced by conservative tradition, tend to think that the main purpose of education is to increase the number and variety of commodities produced. They may include medicine and hygiene, but they will not feel any enthusiasm for literature or

art or philosophy.   Undoubtedly such men
have provided a great part of the driving force
for the attack upon the classical curriculum
established at the renaissance.

I do not think it would be fair to meet this
attitude by the mere assertion that mental goods
are of more value than such as are purely physical.   I believe this assertion to be true, but not
the whole truth.   For, while physical goods
have no very high value, physical evils may be
so bad as to outweigh a great deal of mental
excellence.   Starvation and disease, and the
ever-present fear of them, have overshadowed
the lives of the great majority of mankind since
foresight first became possible.   Most birds die
of starvation, but they are happy when food is
abundant, because they do not think about the
future.   Peasants who have survived a famine
will be perpetually haunted by memory and
apprehension.   Men are willing to toil long
hours for a pittance rather than die, while
animals prefer to snatch pleasure when it is
available, even if death is the penalty.   It has
thus come about that most men have put up
with a life almost wholly devoid of pleasure,
because on any other terms life would be brief.
For the first time in history, it is now possible,
owing to the industrial revolution and its by-
products, to create a world where everybody
shall have a reasonable chance of happiness.

Physical evil can, if we choose, be reduced to very small proportions. It would be possible, by organization and science, to feed and house the whole population of the world, not luxuriously, but sufficiently to prevent great suffering. It would be possible to combat disease, and to make chronic ill-health very rare. It would be possible to prevent the increase of population from outrunning improvements in the food supply. The great terrors which have darkened the sub-conscious mind of the race, bringing cruelty, oppression, and war in their train, could be so much diminished as to be no longer important. All this is of such immeasurable value to human life that we dare not oppose the sort of education which will tend to bring it about. In such an education, applied science will have to be the chief ingredient. Without physics and physiology and psychology, we cannot build the new world. We can build it without Latin and Greek, without Dante and Shakespeare, without Bach and Mozart. That is the great argument in favour of a utilitarian education. I have stated it strongly, because I feel it strongly. Nevertheless, there is another side to the question. What will be the good of the conquest of leisure and health, if no one remembers how to use them? The war against physical evil, like every other war, must not be conducted with such fury as to render men incapable of the arts of peace. What the world possesses of ultimate good must not be allowed to perish in the struggle against evil.

This brings me to the third issue involved in our controversy. Is it true that only useless knowledge is intrinsically valuable? Is it true that any intrinsically valuable knowledge is useless? For my part, I spent in youth a considerable proportion of my time upon Latin and Greek, which I now consider to have been almost completely wasted. Classical knowledge afforded me no help whatever in any of the problems with which I was concerned in later life. Like ninety-nine per cent of those who are taught the classics, I never acquired sufficient proficiency to read them for pleasure. I learned such things as the genitive of "supellex", which I have never been able to forget. This knowledge has no more intrinsic value than the knowledge that there are three feet to a yard; and its utility, to me, has been strictly confined to affording me the present illustration. On the other hand, what I learned of mathematics and science has been not only of immense utility, but also of great intrinsic value, as affording subjects of contemplation and reflection, and touchstones of truth in a deceitful world. This is, of course, in part a personal idiosyncrasy; but I am sure that a capacity to profit by the classics is a still rarer

idiosyncrasy among modern men. France and
Germany also have valuable literatures; their
languages are easily learnt, and are useful in
many practical ways. The case for French and
German, as against Latin and Greek, is therefore overwhelming. Without belittling the
importance of the sort of knowledge which has
no immediate practical utility, I think we may
fairly demand that, except in the education of
specialists, such knowledge shall be given in
ways that do not demand an immense expendi-
ture of time and energy on technical apparatus
such as grammar. The sum of human knowledge and the complexity of human problems
are perpetually increasing; therefore every
generation must overhaul its educational methods if time is to be found for what is new. We
must preserve the balance by means of compro-
mises. The humanistic elements in education
must remain, but they must be sufficiently
simplified to leave room for the other elements
without which the new world rendered possible by science can never be created.

I do not wish to suggest that the humanistic
elements in education are less important than
the utilitarian elements. To know something
of great literature, something of world history,
something of music and painting and architecture, is essential if the life of imagination is to
be fully developed. And it is only through

imagination that men become aware of what the world might be; without it, "progress" would become mechanical and trivial. But science, also, can stimulate the imagination. When I was a boy, astronomy and geology did more for me in this respect than the literatures of England, France and Germany, many of whose masterpieces I read under compulsion without the faintest interest. This is a personal matter: one boy or girl will derive stimulus from one source, another from another. What I suggest is that, where a difficult technique is indispensable to the mastering of a subject, it is better, except in training specialists, that the subject should be useful. In the time of the renaissance, there was little great literature in modern languages; now there is a great deal. Much of the value of the Greek tradition can be conveyed to people who do not know Greek; and as for the Latin tradition, its value is not really very great. I should, therefore, where boys and girls without special aptitudes are concerned, supply the humanistic elements of education in ways not involving a great apparatus of learning; the difficult part of education, in the later years, I should, as a rule, confine to mathematics and science. But I should make exceptions wherever a strong bent or special ability pointed in other directions.   Cast-iron rules are above all things to be avoided.

In a mechanistic civilization, there is grave danger of a crude utilitarianism, which sacrifices the whole æsthetic side of life to what is called "efficiency".   Perhaps I am old-fashioned, but I must confess that I view with alarm the theory that language is merely a means of communication, and not also a vehicle of beauty.   This tendency is world-wide, but naturally it has advanced in America.   In a more or less authoritative book published by the Children's Foundation,[1] I find some remarks on the teaching of English which seem to exemplify the tendency I deplore.   For example:

"Twenty-five years ago pupils learnt from ten to fifteen thousand words, but as a result of investigations carried on during the past two decades, it has been found that the typical graduate of a high school does not need in his school work, and will not need in later life, to spell more than three thousand words at the outside, unless he engages in some technical pursuit, when it may be necessary for him to master a special and technical vocabulary.   The typical American in his correspondence rarely employs more than fifteen hundred different words; many of us never use more than half this num-

[1] "The Child: His Nature and His Needs."   Prepared under the editorial supervision of M. V. O'Shea, Professor of Education, University of Wisconsin, 1924.   I shall allude to this book as "O'Shea".

ber. In view of these facts, the course of spelling in the schools to-day is being constructed
on the principle that the words that will be
actually used in daily life should be mastered
so that they can be spelled automatically, and
the technical and unusual words that were formerly taught but that will probably never be
used are being eliminated" (p. 384).

This seems to me a most singular inversion.
It is still thought that a man should know how
to spell a word he is going to use, although
Shakespeare and Milton could not spell, and the
importance of spelling is purely and solely conventional. But for this trivial purpose there
is a willingness to sacrifice the teaching of a
large vocabulary, without which it is impossible
to write well, or even to understand good writing. The important thing is not to know how
to *spell* words, but how to *use* them; evidently
this was not taught in the days when boys
learned to spell 15,000 words but men only
used 1,500. The way to learn to *use* words is
to read some good literature often and carefully, intensively, not extensively. But careful
reading is positively discouraged. The same
book says of school-children: "They are trained
to read as rapidly as possible so that they will
not be halted in the gaining of meaning by giving attention to separate words, since explicit
awareness of separate words in one's reading

delays and often confuses the process of inter-
preting the thought contained in the reading"
(p. 420). I wonder what pupils so trained
would make of

> Sabrina fair,
> Listen where thou art sitting
> Under the glassy, cool, translucent wave,
> In twisted braids of lilies knitting
> The loose train of thy amber-dropping hair.

No doubt it will be said that the modern man
has no time for such trivialities as the appreciation of great poetry. Yet the very men who
say this are prepared to set aside a great deal of
time in order to teach young men how to kill
each other scientifically. This is surely the
reductio ad absurdum of a utilitarian philosophy.

So far, we have been considering what sort
of knowledge should be imparted. I come
now to a different set of problems, concerned
partly with methods of teaching, partly with
moral education and the training of character.
Here we are no longer concerned with politics,
but with psychology and ethics. Psychology
was, until fairly lately, a merely academic
study, with very little application to practical
affairs. This is all changed now. We have,
for instance, industrial psychology, clinical
psychology, educational psychology, all of the

greatest practical importance. We may hope and expect that the influence of psychology upon our institutions will rapidly increase in the near future. In education, at any rate, its effect has already been great and beneficent.

Let us take first the question of "discipline". The old idea of discipline was simple. A child or boy was ordered to do something he disliked, or abstain from something he liked. When he disobeyed, he suffered physical chastisement, or, in extreme cases, solitary confinement on bread and water. Read, for example, the chapter in "The Fairchild Family" about how little Henry was taught Latin. He was told that he could never hope to become a clergyman unless he learned that language, but in spite of this argument the little boy did not apply himself to his book as earnestly as his father desired. So he was shut up in an attic, given only bread and water, and forbidden to speak to his sisters, who were told that he was in disgrace and they must have nothing to do with him. Nevertheless, one of them brought him some food. The footman told on her, and she got into trouble too. After a certain period in prison, the boy, we are told, began to love Latin and worked assiduously ever after. Contrast with this Chekov's story about his uncle who tried to teach a kitten to catch mice. He brought a mouse into the room where the kitten was, but the kitten's hunting instinct was not yet developed, and it paid no attention to the mouse. So he beat it. The next day the same process was repeated, and the next and the next. At last the Professor became persuaded that it was a stupid kitten, and quite unteachable. In later life, though otherwise normal, it could never see a mouse without sweating in terror and running away. "Like the kitten," Chekov concludes, "I had the honour of being taught Latin by my uncle." These two stories illustrate the old discipline and the modern revolt against it.

But the modern educationist does not simply eschew discipline; he secures it by new methods. On this subject, those who have not studied the new methods are apt to have mistaken ideas. I had always understood that Madame Montessori dispensed with discipline, and I had wondered how she managed a roomful of children. On reading her own account of her methods, I found that discipline still held an important place, and that there was no attempt to dispense with it. On sending my little boy of three to spend his mornings in a Montessori school, I found that he quickly became a more disciplined human being, and that he cheerfully acquiesced in the rules of the school. But he had no feeling whatever of external compulsion: the rules were like the rules of a game, and were obeyed as a means of enjoyment. The old idea was that children could not possibly *wish* to learn, and could only be compelled to learn by terror. It has been found that this was entirely due to lack of skill in pedagogy. By dividing what has to be learnt—for instance, reading and writing—into suitable stages, every stage can be made agreeable to the average child. And when children are doing what they like, there is of course no reason for external discipline. A few simple rules—no child must interfere with another child, no child must have more than one sort of apparatus at a time—are easily apprehended, and felt to be reasonable, so that there is no difficulty in getting them observed. The child thus acquires self-discipline, which consists partly of good habits, partly of the realization, in concrete instances, that it is sometimes worth while to resist an impulse for the sake of some ultimate gain. Everybody has always known that it is easy to obtain this self-discipline in games, but no one had supposed that the acquisition of knowledge could be made sufficiently interesting to bring the same motives into operation. We now know that this is possible, and it will come to be done, not only in the education of infants, but at all stages. I do not pretend that it is easy. The pedagogical discoveries involved have required genius, but the teachers who are to apply them do not require genius. They require only the right sort of training, together with a degree of sympathy and patience which is by no means unusual. The fundamental idea is simple: that the right discipline consists, not in external compulsion, but in habits of mind which lead spontaneously to desirable rather than undesirable activities. What is astonishing is the great success in finding technical methods of embodying this idea in education. For this, Madame Montessori deserves the highest praise.

The change in educational methods has been very much influenced by the decay of the belief in original sin. The traditional view, now nearly extinct, was that we are all born Children of Wrath, with a nature full of wickedness; before there can be any good in us, we have to become Children of Grace, a process much accelerated by frequent castigation. Most moderns can hardly believe how much this theory influenced the education of our fathers and grandfathers. Two quotations from the life of Dr. Arnold by Dean Stanley will show that they are mistaken. Dean Stanley was Dr. Arnold's favourite pupil, the good boy Arthur in "Tom Brown's School Days". He was a cousin of the present writer, who was shown over Westminster Abbey by him as a boy. Dr. Arnold was the great reformer of our public schools, which are viewed as one of the glories of England, and are still conducted largely according to his principles. In discussing Dr. Arnold, therefore, we are dealing, not with something belonging to the remote past, but with something which to this day is efficacious in moulding upper-class Englishmen. Dr. Arnold diminished flogging, retaining it only for the younger boys, and confining it, so his biographer tells us, to "moral offences, such as lying, drinking, and habitual idleness". But when a liberal journal suggested that flogging was a degrading punishment, which ought to be abolished altogether, he was amazingly indignant. He replied in print:

I know well of what feeling this is the expression; it originates in that proud notion of personal independence which is neither reasonable nor Christian, but essentially barbarian. It visited Europe with all the curses of the age of chivalry, and is threatening us now with those of Jacobinism. . . . At an age when it is almost impossible to find a true manly sense of the degradation of guilt or faults, where is the wisdom of encouraging a fantastic sense of the degradation of personal correction? What can be more false, or more adverse to the simplicity, sobriety and humbleness of mind, which are the best ornament of youth, and the best promise of a noble manhood?

The pupils of his disciples, not unnaturally, believe in flogging natives of India when they are deficient in "humbleness of mind".

There is another passage, already quoted in part by Mr. Strachey in "Eminent Victorians", but so apt that I cannot forbear to quote it again. Dr. Arnold was away on a holiday, enjoying the beauties of the Lake of Como. The form his enjoyment took is recorded in a letter to his wife, as follows:

It is almost awful to look at the overwhelming beauty around me, and then think of moral evil; it seems as if heaven and hell, instead of being separated by a great gulf from one another, were absolutely on each other's confines, and indeed not far from every one of us. Might the sense of moral evil be as strong in me as my delight in external beauty, for in a deep sense of moral evil, more perhaps than in anything else, abides a saving knowledge of God! It is not so much to admire moral good; that we may do, and yet not be ourselves conformed to it; but if we really do abhor that which is evil, not the persons in whom evil resides, but the evil which dwelleth in them, and much more manifestly and certainly to our own knowledge, in our own hearts—this is to have the feeling of God and of Christ, and to have our Spirit in sympathy with the Spirit of God. Alas! how easy to see this and say it—how hard to do it and to feel it! Who is sufficient for these things? No one, but he who feels and really laments his own insufficiency. God bless you, my dearest wife, and our beloved children, now and evermore, through Christ Jesus.

It is pathetic to see this naturally kindly gentleman lashing himself into a mood of sadism, in which he can flog little boys without compunction, and all under the impression that he is conforming to the religion of Love. It is pathetic when we consider the deluded individual; but it is tragic when we think of the generations of cruelty that he put into the world by creating an atmosphere of abhorrence of "moral evil", which, it will be remembered, includes habitual idleness in children. I shudder when I think of the wars, the tortures, the oppressions, of which upright men have been guilty, under the impression that they were righteously castigating "moral evil". Mercifully, educators no longer regard little children as limbs of Satan. There is still too much of this view in dealings with adults, particularly in the punishment of crime; but in the nursery and the school it has almost disappeared.

There is an opposite error to Dr. Arnold's, far less pernicious, but still scientifically an error, and that is the belief that children are naturally virtuous, and are only corrupted by the spectacle of their elders' vices. This view is traditionally associated with Rousseau; perhaps he held it in the abstract, but when one reads "Emile" one finds that the pupil stood in need of much moral training before he became the paragon that the system was designed to produce. The fact is that children are not naturally either "good" or "bad". They are born with only reflexes and a few instincts; out of these, by the action of the environment, habits are produced, which may be either healthy or morbid. Which they are to be, depends chiefly upon the wisdom of mothers or nurses, the child's nature being, at first, almost incredibly malleable. In the immense majority of children, there is the raw material of a good citizen, and also the raw material of a criminal. Scientific psychology shows that flogging on weekdays and sermons on Sundays do not constitute the ideal technique for the production of virtue. But it is not to be inferred that there is no technique for this purpose. It is difficult to resist Samuel Butler's view that the educators of former times took a pleasure in torturing children; otherwise it is hard to see how they can have persisted so long in inflicting useless misery. It is not difficult to make a healthy child happy, and most children will be healthy if their minds and bodies are properly tended. Happiness in childhood is absolutely necessary to the production of the best type of human

being.   Habitual idleness, which Dr. Arnold
regarded as a form of "moral evil", will not
exist if the child is made to feel that its education is teaching it something worth knowing.[2]
But if the knowledge imparted is worthless,
and those who impart it appear as cruel tyrants,
the child will naturally behave like Chekov's
kitten.   The spontaneous wish to learn, which
every normal child possesses, as shown in its
efforts to walk and talk, should be the driving-
force in education.   The substitution of this
driving-force for the rod is one of the great
advances of our time.

This brings me to the last point which I wish
to notice in this preliminary survey of modern
tendencies—I mean, the greater attention paid
to infancy.   This is closely connected with the
change in our ideas as to the training of character.   The old idea was that virtue depends
essentially upon *will*: we were supposed to be
full of bad desires, which we controlled by an
abstract faculty of volition.   It was apparently
regarded as impossible to root out bad desires;
all we could do was to control them.   The situation was exactly analogous to that of the
criminal and the police.   No one supposed that
a society without would-be criminals was pos-

[2] Probably many of Dr. Arnold's pupils suffered from adenoids,
for which medical men do not usually prescribe flogging, although
they cause habitual idleness.

sible; the most that could be done was to have such an efficient police force that most people would be afraid to commit crimes, and the few exceptions would be caught and punished. The modern psychological criminologist is not content with this view; he believes that the impulse to crime could, in most cases, be prevented from developing by suitable education. And what applies to society applies also to the individual. Children, especially, wish to be liked by their elders and their companions; they have, as a rule, impulses which can be developed in good or bad directions according to the situations in which they find themselves. Moreover they are at an age at which the formation of new habits is still easy; and good habits can make a great part of virtue almost automatic. On the other hand, the older type of virtue, which left bad desires rampant, and merely used will-power to check their manifestations, has been found to afford a far from satisfactory method of controlling bad conduct. The bad desires, like a river which has been dammed, find some other outlet which has escaped the watchful eye of the will. The man who, in youth, would have liked to murder his father, finds satisfaction later on in flogging his son, under the impression that he is chastising "moral evil". Theories which justify cruelty almost always have their source in some desire diverted by the will from its natural channel, driven underground, and at last emerging unrecognized as hatred of sin or something equally respectable. The control of bad desires by the will, therefore, though necessary on occasion, is inadequate as a technique of virtue.

These considerations bring us to the province of psycho-analysis. There is much in the detail of psycho-analysis which I find fantastic, and not supported by adequate evidence. But the general method appears to me very important, and essential to the creation of right methods of moral training. The importance which many psycho-analysts attach to early infancy appears to me exaggerated; they sometimes talk as if character were irrevocably fixed by the time a child is three years old. This, I am sure, is not the case. But the fault is a fault on the right side. Infant psychology was neglected in the past; indeed, the intellectualist methods in vogue made it almost impossible. Take such a matter as sleep. All mothers wish their children to sleep, because it is both healthy and convenient when they do. They had developed a certain technique: rocking the cradle and singing lullabys. It was left for males who investigated the matter scientifically to discover that this technique is ideally wrong, for though it is likely to succeed on any given day, it creates bad habits. Every child loves to be made a fuss of, because its sense of self-importance is gratified. If it finds that by not sleeping it secures attention, it will soon learn to adopt this method. The result is equally damaging to health and character. The great thing here is the formation of habit: the association of the cot with sleep. If this association has been adequately produced, the child will not lie awake unless it is ill or in pain. But the production of the association requires a certain amount of discipline; it is not to be achieved by mere indulgence, since that causes pleasurable associations with lying awake. Similar considerations apply to the formation of other good and bad habits. This whole study is still in its infancy, but its importance is already very great, and almost sure to become greater. It is clear that education of character must begin at birth, and requires a reversal of much of the practice of nurses and ignorant mothers. It is also clear that definite instruction can begin earlier than was formerly thought, because it can be made pleasant and no strain upon the infant's powers of attention. In both these respects educational theory has been radically transformed in recent years, with beneficent effects which are likely to become more and more evident as the years go by.   Accordingly I shall begin, in what follows, with a fairly detailed consideration of the training of character in infancy, before discussing the instruction to be given in later years.

CHAPTER II

THE AIMS OF EDUCATION

BEFORE considering how to educate, it is well to be clear as to the sort of result which we wish to achieve. Dr. Arnold wanted "humbleness of mind", a quality not possessed by Aristotle's "magnanimous man". Nietzsche's ideal is not that of Christianity. No more is Kant's: for while Christ enjoins love, Kant teaches that no action of which love is the motive can be truly virtuous. And even people who agree as to the ingredients of a good character may differ as to their relative importance. One man will emphasize courage, another learning, another kindliness, and another rectitude. One man, like the elder Brutus, will put duty to the State above family affection; another, like Confucius, will put family affection first. All these divergences will produce differences as to education. We must have some conception of the kind of person we wish to produce, before we can have any definite opinion as to the education which we consider best.

Of course an educator may be foolish, in the sense that he produces results other than those at which he was aiming.   Uriah Heep was the outcome of lessons in humility at a Charity School, which had had an effect quite different from what was intended.   But in the main the ablest educators have been fairly successful. Take as examples the Chinese literati, the modern Japanese, the Jesuits, Dr. Arnold, and the men who direct the policy of the American public schools.   All these, in their various ways, have been highly successful.   The results aimed at in the different cases were utterly different, but in the main the results were achieved.   It may be worth while to spend a few moments on these different systems, before attempting to decide what we should ourselves regard as the aims which education should have in view.

Traditional Chinese education was, in some respects, very similar to that of Athens in its best days.   Athenian boys were made to learn Homer by heart from beginning to end; Chinese boys were made to learn the Confucian classics with similar thoroughness.   Athenians were taught a kind of reverence for the gods which consisted in outward observances, and placed no barrier in the way of free intellectual speculation.   Similarly the Chinese were taught certain rites connected with ancestor-worship, but were by no means obliged to have the beliefs which the rites would seem to imply. An easy and elegant scepticism was the attitude expected of an educated adult: anything might be discussed, but it was a trifle vulgar to reach very positive conclusions. Opinions should be such as could be discussed pleasantly at dinner, not such as men would fight for. Carlyle calls Plato "a lordly Athenian gentleman, very much at his ease in Zion". This characteristic of being "at his ease in Zion" is also found in Chinese sages, and is, as a rule, absent from the sages produced by Christian civilizations, except when, like Goethe, they have deeply imbibed the spirit of Hellenism. The Athenians and the Chinese alike wished to enjoy life, and had a conception of enjoyment which was refined by an exquisite sense of beauty.

There were, however, great differences between the two civilizations, owing to the fact that, broadly speaking, the Greeks were energetic and the Chinese were lazy. The Greeks devoted their energies to art and science and mutual extermination, in all of which they achieved unprecedented success. Politics and patriotism afforded practical outlets for Greek energy: when a politician was ousted, he led a band of exiles to attack his native city. When a Chinese official was disgraced, he retired to the hills and wrote poems on the pleasures of

country life. Accordingly the Greek civilization destroyed itself, but the Chinese civilization could only be destroyed from without.
These differences, however, seem not wholly
attributable to education, since Confucianism
in Japan never produced the indolent cultured
scepticism which characterized the Chinese
literati, except in the Kyoto nobility, who
formed a kind of Faubourg Saint Germain.

Chinese education produced stability and art;
it failed to produce progress or science. Perhaps this may be taken as what is to be expected
of scepticism. Passionate beliefs produce
either progress or disaster, not stability. Science, even when it attacks traditional beliefs,
has beliefs of its own, and can scarcely flourish
in an atmosphere of literary scepticism. In a
pugnacious world which has been unified by
modern inventions, energy is needed for national self-preservation. And without science,
democracy is impossible: the Chinese civilization was confined to the small percentage of
educated men, and the Greek civilization was
based on slavery. For these reasons, the traditional education of China is not suited to the
modern world, and has been abandoned by the
Chinese themselves. Cultivated eighteenth-
century gentlemen, who in some respects re-
sembled Chinese literati, have become impossible for the same reasons.

Modern Japan affords the clearest illustration of a tendency which is prominent among all the Great Powers—the tendency to make national greatness the supreme purpose of education. The aim of Japanese education is to produce citizens who shall be devoted to the State through the training of their passions, and useful to it through the knowledge they have acquired. I cannot sufficiently praise the skill with which this double purpose has been pursued. Ever since the advent of Commodore Perry's squadron, the Japanese have been in a situation in which self-preservation was very difficult; their success affords a justification of their methods, unless we are to hold that self-preservation itself may be culpable. But only a desperate situation could have justified their educational methods, which would have been culpable in any nation not in imminent peril. The Shinto religion, which must not be called in question even by university professors, involves history which is just as dubious as Genesis; the Dayton trial pales into insignificance beside the theological tyranny in Japan. There is an equal ethical tyranny: nationalism, filial piety, Mikado-worship, etc., must not be called in question, and therefore many kinds of progress are scarcely possible. The great danger of a cast-iron system of this sort is that it may provoke revolution as the sole method of progress. This danger is real, though not immediate, and is largely caused by the educational system.

We have thus in modern Japan a defect opposite to that of ancient China. Whereas the Chinese literati were too sceptical and lazy, the products of Japanese education are likely to be too dogmatic and energetic. Neither acquiescence in scepticism nor acquiescence in dogma is what education should produce. What it should produce is a belief that knowledge is attainable in a measure, though with difficulty; that much of what passes for knowledge at any given time is likely to be more or less mistaken, but that the mistakes can be rectified by care and industry. In acting upon our beliefs, we should be very cautious where a small error would mean disaster; nevertheless it is upon our beliefs that we must act. This state of mind is rather difficult: it requires a high degree of intellectual culture without emotional atrophy. But though difficult it is not impossible; it is in fact the scientific temper. Knowledge, like other good things, is difficult, but not impossible; the dogmatist forgets the difficulty, the sceptic denies the possibility. Both are mistaken, and their errors, when wide-spread, produce social disaster.

The Jesuits, like the modern Japanese, made the mistake of subordinating education to the welfare of an institution—in their case, the Catholic Church. They were not concerned primarily with the good of the particular pupil, but with making him a means to the good of the Church. If we accept their theology, we cannot blame them: to save souls from hell is more important than any merely terrestrial concern, and is only to be achieved by the Catholic Church. But those who do not accept this dogma will judge Jesuit education by its results. These results, it is true, were sometimes quite as undesired as Uriah Heep: Voltaire was a product of Jesuit methods. But on the whole, and for a long time, the intended results were achieved: the counter-reformation, and the collapse of Protestantism in France, must be largely attributed to Jesuit efforts. To achieve these ends, they made art sentimental, thought superficial, and morals loose; in the end, the French Revolution was needed to sweep away the harm that they had done. In education, their crime was that they were not actuated by love of their pupils, but by ulterior ends.

Dr. Arnold's system, which has remained in force in English public schools to the present day, had another defect, namely that it was aristocratic. The aim was to train men for positions of authority and power, whether at home or in distant parts of the empire. An aristocracy, if it is to survive, needs certain virtues; these were to be imparted at school. The product was to be energetic, stoical, physically fit, possessed of certain unalterable beliefs, with high standards of rectitude, and convinced that it had an important mission in the world. To a surprising extent, these results were achieved. Intellect was sacrificed to them, because intellect might produce doubt. Sympathy was sacrificed, because it might interfere with governing "inferior" races or classes. Kindliness was sacrificed for the sake of toughness; imagination, for the sake of firmness. In an unchanging world, the result might have been a permanent aristocracy, possessing the merits and defects of the Spartans. But aristocracy is out of date, and subject populations will no longer obey even the most wise and virtuous rulers. The rulers are driven into brutality, and brutality further encourages revolt. The complexity of the modern world increasingly requires intelligence, and Dr. Arnold sacrificed intelligence to "virtue". The battle of Waterloo may have been won on the playing-fields of Eton, but the British Empire is being lost there. The modern world needs a different type, with more imaginative sympathy, more intellectual suppleness, less belief in bulldog courage and more belief in technical knowledge. The administrator of the future must be the servant of free citizens, not the benevolent ruler of admiring subjects. The aristocratic tradition embedded in British higher education is its bane. Perhaps this tradition can be eliminated gradually; perhaps the older educational institutions will be found incapable of adapting themselves. As to that, I do not venture an opinion.

The American public schools achieve successfully a task never before attempted on a large scale: the task of transforming a heterogeneous selection of mankind into a homogeneous nation. This is done so ably, and is on the whole such a beneficent work, that on the balance great praise is due to those who accomplish it. But America, like Japan, is placed in a peculiar situation, and what the special circumstances justify is not necessarily an ideal to be followed everywhere and always. America has had certain advantages and certain difficulties. Among the advantages were: a higher standard of wealth; freedom from the danger of defeat in war; comparative absence of cramping traditions inherited from the Middle Ages. Immigrants found in America a generally diffused sentiment of democracy and an advanced stage of industrial technique. These, I think, are the two chief reasons why almost all of them came to admire America more than their native countries. But actual immigrants, as a rule, retain a dual patriotism: in European struggles they continue to take passionately the side of the nation to which they originally belonged. Their children, on the contrary, lose all loyalty to the country from which their parents have come, and become merely and simply Americans. The attitude of the parents is attributable to the general merits of America; that of the children is very largely determined by their school education. It is only the contribution of the school that concerns us.

In so far as the school can rely upon the genuine merits of America, there is no need to associate the teaching of American patriotism with the inculcation of false standards. But where the Old World is superior to the New, it becomes necessary to instil a contempt for genuine excellences. The intellectual level in Western Europe and the artistic level in Eastern Europe are, on the whole, higher than in America. Throughout Western Europe, except in Spain and Portugal, there is less theological superstition than in America. In almost all European countries the individual is less subject to herd domination than in America: his inner freedom is greater even where his political freedom is less. In these respects, the American public schools do harm. The harm

is essential to the teaching of an exclusive
American patriotism. The harm, as with the
Japanese and the Jesuits, comes from regarding
the pupils as means to an end, not as ends in
themselves. The teacher should love his children better than his State or his Church; otherwise he is not an ideal teacher.

When I say that pupils should be regarded
as ends, not as means, I may be met by the
retort that, after all, everybody is more important as a means than as an end. What a man
is as an end perishes when he dies; what he
produces as a means continues to the end of
time. We cannot deny this, but we can deny
the consequences deduced from it. A man's
importance as a means may be for good or for
evil; the remote effects of human actions are so
uncertain that a wise man will tend to dismiss
them from his calculations. Broadly speaking,
good men have good effects, and bad men bad
effects. This, of course, is not an invariable
law of nature. A bad man may murder a
tyrant because he has committed crimes which
the tyrant intends to punish; the effects of his
act may be good, though he and his act are bad.
Nevertheless, as a broad general rule, a community of men and women who are intrinsically
excellent will have better effects than one composed of people who are ignorant and malevo-

lent. Apart from such considerations, children and young people feel instinctively the difference between those who genuinely wish them well and those who regard them merely as raw material for some scheme. Neither character nor intelligence will develop as well or as freely where the teacher is deficient in love; and love of this kind consists essentially in *feeling* the child as an end. We all have this feeling about ourselves: we desire good things for ourselves without first demanding a proof that some great purpose will be furthered by our obtaining them. Every ordinarily affectionate parent feels the same sort of thing about his or her children. Parents want their children to grow, to be strong and healthy, to do well at school, and so on, in just the same way in which they want things for themselves; no effort of self-denial and no abstract principle of justice is involved in taking trouble about such matters. This parental instinct is not always strictly confined to one's own children. In its diffused form, it must exist in anyone who is to be a good teacher of little boys and girls. As the pupils grow older, it grows less important. But only those who possess it can be trusted to draw up schemes of education. Those who regard it as one of the purposes of male education to produce men willing to kill and be killed for frivolous reasons are clearly deficient in diffused parental feeling; yet they control education in all civilized countries except Denmark and China.

But it is not enough that the educator should love the young; it is necessary also that he should have a right conception of human excellence. Cats teach their kittens to catch mice and play with them; militarists do likewise with the human young. The cat loves the kitten, but not the mouse; the militarist may love his own son, but not the sons of his country's enemies. Even those who love all mankind may err through a wrong conception of the good life. I shall try, therefore, before going any further, to give an idea of what I consider excellent in men and women, quite without regard to practicality, or to the educational methods by which it might be brought into being. Such a picture will help us afterwards, when we come to consider the details of education; we shall know the direction in which we wish to move.

We must first make a distinction: some qualities are desirable in a certain proportion of mankind, others are desirable universally. We want artists, but we also want men of science. We want great administrators, but we also want ploughmen and millers and bakers. The qualities which produce a man of great eminence in some one direction are often such as might be undesirable if they were universal. Shelley describes the day's work of a poet as follows:

> He will watch from dawn to gloom
> The lake-reflected sun illume
> The honey-bees in the ivy bloom,
> Nor heed nor see what things they be.

These habits are praiseworthy in a poet, but not—shall we say—in a postman. We cannot therefore frame our education with a view to giving every one the temperament of a poet. But some characteristics are universally desirable, and it is these alone that I shall consider at this stage.

I make no distinction whatever between male and female excellence. A certain amount of occupational training is desirable for a woman who is to have the care of babies, but that only involves the same sort of difference as there is between a farmer and a miller. It is in no degree fundamental, and does not demand consideration at our present level.

I will take four characteristics which seem to me jointly to form the basis of an ideal character: vitality, courage, sensitiveness, and intelligence. I do not suggest that this list is complete, but I think it carries us a good way. Moreover I firmly believe that, by proper physical, emotional and intellectual care of the young, these qualities could all be made very common. I shall consider each in turn.

Vitality is rather a physiological than a mental characteristic; it is presumably always present where there is perfect health, but it tends to ebb with advancing years, and gradually dwindles to nothing in old age. In vigorous children it quickly rises to a maximum before they reach school age, and then tends to be diminished by education. Where it exists, there is pleasure in feeling alive, quite apart from any specific pleasant circumstance. It heightens pleasures and diminishes pains. It makes it easy to take an interest in whatever occurs, and thus promotes objectivity, which is an essential of sanity. Human beings are prone to become absorbed in themselves, unable to be interested in what they see and hear or in anything outside their own skins. This is a great misfortune to themselves, since it entails at best boredom and at worst melancholia; it is also a fatal barrier to usefulness, except in very exceptional cases. Vitality promotes interest in the outside world; it also promotes the power of hard work. Moreover it is a safeguard against envy, because it makes one's own existence pleasant. As envy is one of the great sources of human misery, this is a very important merit in vitality. Many bad qualities are of course compatible with vitality—

for example, those of a healthy tiger. And many of the best qualities are compatible with its absence: Newton and Locke, for example, had very little. Both these men, however, had irritabilities and envies from which better health would have set them free. Probably the whole of Newton's controversy with Leibniz, which ruined English mathematics for over a hundred years, would have been avoided if Newton had been robust and able to enjoy ordinary pleasures. In spite of its limitations, therefore, I reckon vitality among the qualities which it is important that all men should possess.

Courage—the second quality on our list— has several forms, and all of them are complex. Absence of fear is one thing, and the power of controlling fear is another. And absence of fear, in turn, is one thing when the fear is rational, another when it is irrational. Absence of irrational fear is clearly good; so is the power of controlling fear. But absence of rational fear is a matter as to which debate is possible. However, I shall postpone this question until I have said something about the other forms of courage.

Irrational fear plays an extraordinarily large part in the instinctive emotional life of most people. In its pathological forms, as persecution mania, anxiety complex, or what not, it is

treated by alienists. But in milder forms it is
common among those who are considered sane.
It may be a general feeling that there
are dangers about, more correctly termed
"anxiety", or a specific dread of things that are
not dangerous, such as mice or spiders.[1] It
used to be supposed that many fears were instinctive, but this is now questioned by most
investigators. There are apparently a few
instinctive fears—for instance, of loud noises—
but the great majority arise either from experience or from suggestion. Fear of the dark,
for example, seems to be entirely due to suggestion. Most vertebrates, there is reason to
think, do not feel instinctive fear of their natural enemies, but catch this emotion from their
elders. When human beings bring them up by
hand, the fears usual among the species are
found to be absent. But fear is exceedingly
infectious: children catch it from their elders
even when their elders are not aware of having
shown it. Timidity in mothers or nurses is
very quickly imitated by children through suggestion. Hitherto, men have thought it attractive in women to be full of irrational terrors,
because it gave men a chance to seem protective
without incurring any real danger. But the
sons of these men have acquired the terrors

[1] On fear and anxiety in childhood, see *e.g.* William Stern,
"Psychology of Early Childhood", Chap. XXXV. (Henry Holt,
1924).

from their mothers, and have had to be afterwards trained to regain a courage which they need never have lost if their fathers had not desired to despise their mothers. The harm that has been done by the subjection of women is incalculable; this matter of fear affords only one incidental illustration.

I am not at the moment discussing the methods by which fear and anxiety may be minimized; that is a matter which I shall consider later. There is, however, one question which arises at this stage, namely: can we be content to deal with fear by means of repression, or must we find some more radical cure? Traditionally, aristocracies have been trained not to show fear, while subject nations, classes, and sexes have been encouraged to remain cowardly. The test of courage has been crudely behavioristic: a man must not run away in battle; he must be proficient in "manly" sports; he must retain self-command in fires, shipwrecks, earthquakes, etc. He must not merely do the right thing, but he must avoid turning pale, or trembling, or gasping for breath, or giving any other easily observed sign of fear. All this I regard as of great importance: I should wish to see courage cultivated in all nations, in all classes, and in both sexes. But when the method adopted is repressive, it entails the evils always associated with that practice. Shame and disgrace have always been potent weapons in producing the appearance of courage; but in fact they merely cause a conflict of terrors, in which it is hoped that the dread of public condemnation will be the stronger. "Always speak the truth except when something frightens you" was a maxim taught to me in childhood. I cannot admit the exception. Fear should be overcome not only in action, but in feeling; and not only in conscious feeling, but in the unconscious as well. The purely external victory over fear, which satisfies the aristocratic code, leaves the impulse operative underground, and produces evil twisted reactions which are not recognized as the offspring of terror. I am not thinking of "shell shock", in which the connection with fear is obvious. I am thinking rather of the whole system of oppression and cruelty by which dominant castes seek to retain their ascendancy. When recently in Shanghai a British officer ordered a number of unarmed Chinese students to be shot in the back without warning, he was obviously actuated by terror just as much as a soldier who runs away in battle. But military aristocracies are not sufficiently intelligent to trace such actions to their psychological source; they regard them rather as showing firmness and a proper spirit.

From the point of view of psychology and

physiology, fear and rage are closely analogous emotions: the man who feels rage is not possessed of the highest kind of courage. The cruelty invariably displayed in suppressing negro insurrections, communist rebellions, and other threats to aristocracy, is an offshoot of cowardice, and deserves the same contempt as is bestowed upon the more obvious forms of that vice. I believe that it is possible so to educate ordinary men and women that they shall be able to live without fear. Hitherto, only a few heroes and saints have achieved such a life; but what they have done others could do if they were shown the way.

For the kind of courage which does not consist in repression, a number of factors must be combined. To begin with the humblest: health and vitality are very helpful, though not indispensable. Practice and skill in dangerous situations are very desirable. But when we come to consider, not courage in this and that respect, but universal courage, something more fundamental is wanted. What is wanted is a combination of self-respect with an impersonal outlook on life. To begin with self-respect: some men live from within, while others are mere mirrors of what is felt and said by their neighbours. The latter can never have true courage: they must have admiration, and are haunted by the fear of losing it. The teaching of "humility", which used to be thought desirable, was the means of producing a perverted form of this same vice. "Humility" suppressed self-respect, but not the desire for the respect of others; it merely made nominal self-abasement the means of acquiring credit. Thus it produced hypocrisy and falsification of instinct. Children were taught unreasoning submission, and proceeded to exact it when they grew up; it was said that only those who have learned to obey know how to command. What I suggest is that no one should learn how to obey, and no one should attempt to command. I do not mean, of course, that there should not be leaders in co-operative enterprises; but their authority should be like that of a captain of a football team, which is suffered voluntarily in order to achieve a common purpose. Our purposes should be our own, not the result of external authority; and our purposes should never be forcibly imposed upon others. This is what I mean when I say no one should command and no one should obey.

There is one thing more required for the highest courage, and that is what I called just now an impersonal outlook on life. The man whose hopes and fears are all centred upon himself can hardly view death with equanimity, since it extinguishes his whole emotional universe. Here, again, we are met by a tradition urging the cheap and easy way of repression: the saint must learn to renounce Self, must mortify the flesh and forego instinctive joys. This can be done, but its consequences are bad. Having renounced pleasure for himself, the ascetic saint renounces it for others also, which is easier. Envy persists underground, and leads him to the view that suffering is ennobling, and may therefore be legitimately inflicted. Hence arises a complete inversion of values: what is good is thought bad, and what is bad is thought good. The source of all the harm is that the good life has been sought in obedience to a negative imperative, not in broadening and developing natural desires and instincts. There are certain things in human nature which take us beyond Self without effort. The commonest of these is love, more particularly parental love, which in some is so generalized as to embrace the whole human race. Another is knowledge. There is no reason to suppose that Galileo was particularly benevolent, yet he lived for an end which was not defeated by his death. Another is art. But in fact every interest in something outside a man's own body makes his life to that degree impersonal. For this reason, paradoxical as it may seem, a man of wide and vivid interests finds less difficulty in leaving life than is experienced by some miserable hypochondriac whose interests are bounded by his own ailments. Thus the perfection of courage is found in the man of many interests, who *feels* his ego to be but a small part of the world, not through despising himself, but through valuing much that is not himself. This can hardly happen except where instinct is free and intelligence is active. From the union of the two grows a comprehensiveness of outlook unknown both to the voluptuary and to the ascetic; and to such an outlook personal death appears a trivial matter. Such courage is positive and instinctive, not negative and repressive. It is courage in this positive sense that I regard as one of the major ingredients in a perfect character.

Sensitiveness, the third quality in our list, is in a sense a corrective of mere courage. Courageous behaviour is easier for a man who fails to apprehend dangers, but such courage may often be foolish. We cannot regard as satisfactory any way of acting which is dependent upon ignorance or forgetfulness: the fullest possible knowledge and realization are an essential part of what is desirable. The cognitive aspect, however, comes under the head of intelligence; sensitiveness, in the sense in which I am using the term, belongs to the emotions. A purely theoretical definition would be that a person is emotionally sensitive when many stimuli produce emotions in him;

but taken thus broadly the quality is not necessarily a good one. If sensitiveness is to be good, the emotional reaction must be in some sense *appropriate*: mere intensity is not what is needed. The quality I have in mind is that of being affected pleasurably or the reverse by many things, and by the right things. What are the right things, I shall try to explain. The first step, which most children take at the age of about five months, is to pass beyond mere pleasures of sensation, such as food and warmth, to the pleasure of social approbation. This pleasure, as soon as it has arisen, develops very rapidly: every child loves praise and hates blame. Usually the wish to be thought well of remains one of the dominant motives throughout life. It is certainly very valuable as a stimulus to pleasant behaviour, and as a restraint upon impulses of greed. If we were wiser in our admirations, it might be much more valuable. But so long as the most admired heroes are those who have killed the greatest number of people, love of admiration cannot alone be adequate to the good life.

The next stage in the development of a desirable form of sensitiveness is sympathy. There is a purely physical sympathy: a very young child will cry because a brother or sister is crying. This, I suppose, affords the basis for the further developments. The two enlargements that are needed are: first, to feel sympathy even when the sufferer is not an object of special affection; secondly, to feel it when the suffering is merely known to be occurring, not sensibly present. The second of these enlargements depends mainly upon intelligence. It may only go so far as sympathy with suffering which is portrayed vividly and touchingly, as in a good novel; it may, on the other hand, go so far as to enable a man to be moved emotionally by statistics. This capacity for abstract sympathy is as rare as it is important. Almost everybody is deeply affected when some one he loves suffers from cancer. Most people are moved when they see the sufferings of unknown patients in hospitals. Yet when they read that the death-rate from cancer is such-and-such, they are as a rule only moved to momentary personal fear lest they or some one dear to them should acquire the disease. The same is true of war: people think it dreadful when their son or brother is mutilated, but they do not think it a million times as dreadful that a million people should be mutilated. A man who is full of kindliness in all personal dealings may derive his income from incitement to war or from the torture of children in "backward" countries. All these familiar phenomena are due to the fact that sympathy is not stirred, in most people, by a merely abstract stimulus. A large proportion of the evils in the modern world would cease if this could be remedied. Science has greatly increased our power of affecting the lives of distant people, without increasing our sympathy for them. Suppose you are a shareholder in a company which manufactures cotton in Shanghai. You may be a busy man, who has merely followed financial advice in making the investment; neither Shanghai nor cotton interests you, but only your dividends. Yet you become part of the force leading to massacres of innocent people, and your dividends would disappear if little children were not forced into unnatural and dangerous toil. You do not mind, because you have never seen the children, and an abstract stimulus cannot move you. That is the fundamental reason why large-scale industrialism is so cruel, and why oppression of subject races is tolerated. An education producing sensitiveness to abstract stimuli would make such things impossible.

Cognitive sensitiveness, which should also be included, is practically the same thing as a habit of observation, and this is more naturally considered in connection with intelligence. Æsthetic sensitiveness raises a number of problems which I do not wish to discuss at this stage. I will therefore pass on to the last of the four qualities we enumerated, namely, intelligence.

One of the great defects of traditional morality has been the low estimate it placed upon intelligence. The Greeks did not err in this respect, but the Church led men to think that nothing matters except virtue, and virtue consists in abstinence from a certain list of actions arbitrarily labelled "sin". So long as this attitude persists, it is impossible to make men realize that intelligence does more good than an artificial conventional "virtue". When I speak of intelligence, I include both actual knowledge and receptivity to knowledge. The two are, in fact, closely connected. Ignorant adults are unteachable; on such matters as hygiene or diet, for example, they are totally incapable of believing what science has to say. The more a man has learnt, the easier it is for him to learn still more—always assuming that he has not been taught in a spirit of dogmatism. Ignorant people have never been compelled to change their mental habits, and have stiffened into an unchangeable attitude. It is not only that they are credulous where they should be sceptical; it is just as much that they are in-credulous where they should be receptive. No doubt the word "intelligence" properly signifies rather an aptitude for acquiring knowledge than knowledge already acquired; but I do not think this aptitude is acquired except by exercise, any more than the aptitude of a pianist or an acrobat. It is, of course, possible to impart information in ways that do not train intelligence; it is not only possible, but easy, and frequently done. But I do not believe that it is possible to train intelligence without imparting information, or at any rate causing knowledge to be acquired. And without intelligence our complex modern world cannot subsist; still less can it make progress. I regard the cultivation of intelligence, therefore, as one of the major purposes of education. This might seem a commonplace, but in fact it is not. The desire to instil what are regarded as correct beliefs has made educationists too often indifferent to the training of intelligence. To make this clear, it is necessary to define intelligence a little more closely, so as to discover the mental habits which it requires. For this purpose I shall consider only the aptitude for acquiring knowledge, not the store of actual knowledge which might legitimately be included in the definition of intelligence.

The instinctive foundation of the intellectual life is curiosity, which is found among animals in its elementary forms. Intelligence demands an alert curiosity, but it must be of a certain kind. The sort that leads village neighbours to try to peer through curtains after dark has no very high value. The wide-spread interest in gossip is inspired, not by a love of knowledge, but by malice: no one gossips about other people's secret virtues, but only about their secret vices. Accordingly most gossip is untrue, but care is taken not to verify it. Our neighbours' sins, like the consolations of religion, are so agreeable that we do not stop to scrutinize the evidence closely. Curiosity properly so called, on the other hand, is inspired by a genuine love of knowledge. You may see this impulse, in a moderately pure form, at work in a cat which has been brought to a strange room, and proceeds to smell every corner and every piece of furniture. You will see it also in children, who are passionately interested when a drawer or cupboard, usually closed, is open for their inspection. Animals, machines, thunderstorms, and all forms of manual work, arouse the curiosity of children, whose thirst for knowledge puts the most intelligent adult to shame. This impulse grows weaker with advancing years, until at last what is unfamiliar inspires only disgust, with no desire for a closer acquaintance. This is the stage at which people announce that the country is going to the dogs, and that "things are not what they were in my young days". The thing which is not the same as it was in that far-off time is the speaker's curiosity. And with the death of curiosity we may reckon that active intelligence, also, has died.

But although curiosity lessens in intensity and in extent after childhood, it may for a long time improve in quality. Curiosity about general propositions shows a higher level of intelligence than curiosity about particular facts; broadly speaking, the higher the order of generality the greater is the intelligence involved. (This rule, however, must not be taken too strictly.) Curiosity dissociated from personal advantage shows a higher development than curiosity connected (say) with a chance of food. The cat that sniffs in a new room is not a wholly disinterested scientific inquirer, but probably also wants to find out whether there are mice about. Perhaps it is not quite correct to say that curiosity is best when it is disinterested, but rather that it is best when the connection with other interests is not direct and obvious, but discoverable only by means of a certain degree of intelligence. This point, however, it is not necessary for us to decide.

If curiosity is to be fruitful, it must be associated with a certain technique for the acquisition of knowledge. There must be habits of observation, belief in the possibility of knowledge, patience and industry. These things will develop of themselves, given the original fund of curiosity and the proper intellectual education. But since our intellectual life is only a part of our activity, and since curiosity is perpetually coming into conflict with other passions, there is need of certain intellectual virtues, such as open-mindedness. We become impervious to new truth both from habit and from desire: we find it hard to disbelieve what we have emphatically believed for a number of years, and also what ministers to self-esteem or any other fundamental passion. Open-mindedness should therefore be one of the qualities that education aims at producing. At present, this is only done to a very limited extent, as is illustrated by the following paragraph from "The Daily Herald", July 31, 1925:

A special committee, appointed to inquire into the allegations of the subversion of children's minds in Bootle schools by their school teachers, has placed its findings before the Bootle Borough Council. The Committee was of opinion that the allegations were substantiated, but the Council deleted the word "substantiated", and stated that "the allegations gave cause for reasonable inquiry". A recommendation made by the Committee, and adopted by the Council, was that in future appointments of teachers, they shall undertake to train the scholars in habits of reverence towards God and religion, and of respect for the civil and religious institutions of the country.

Thus whatever may happen elsewhere, there is to be no open-mindedness in Bootle. It is hoped that the Borough Council will shortly send a deputation to Dayton, Tennessee, to obtain further light upon the best methods of carrying out their programme. But perhaps that is unnecessary. From the wording of the resolution, it would seem as if Bootle needed no instruction in obscurantism.

Courage is essential to intellectual probity, as well as to physical heroism. The real world is more unknown than we like to think; from the first day of life we practise precarious inductions, and confound our mental habits with laws of external nature. All sorts of intellectual systems—Christianity, Socialism, Patriotism, etc.—are ready, like orphan asylums, to give safety in return for servitude. A free mental life cannot be as warm and comfortable and sociable as a life enveloped in a creed: only a creed can give the feeling of a cosy fireside while the winter storms are raging without.

This brings us to a somewhat difficult question: to what extent should the good life be emancipated from the herd? I hesitate to use the phrase "herd instinct", because there are controversies as to its correctness. But, however interpreted, the phenomena which it describes are familiar. We like to stand well with those whom we feel to be the group with which

we wish to co-operate—our family, our neighbours, our colleagues, our political party, or
our nation. This is natural, because we cannot
obtain any of the pleasures of life without co-
operation. Moreover, emotions are infectious,
especially when they are felt by many people at
once. Very few people can be present at an
excited meeting without getting excited: if they
are opponents, their opposition becomes excited.
And to most people such opposition is only
possible if they can derive support from the
thought of a different crowd in which they will
win approbation. That is why the Communion
of Saints has afforded such comfort to the persecuted. Are we to acquiesce in this desire for
co-operation with a crowd, or shall our education try to weaken it? There are arguments
on both sides, and the right answer must consist
in finding a just proportion, not in a wholehearted decision for either party.

I think myself that the desire to please and
to co-operate should be strong and normal, but
should be capable of being overcome by other
desires on certain important occasions. The
desirability of a wish to please has already been
considered in connection with sensitiveness.
Without it, we should all be boors, and all social
groups, from the family upwards, would be
impossible. Education of young children
would be very difficult if they did not desire the

good opinion of their parents. The contagious character of emotions also has its uses, when the contagion is from a wiser person to a more foolish one. But in the case of panic fear and panic rage it is of course the very reverse of useful. Thus the question of emotional receptivity is by no means simple. Even in purely intellectual matters, the issue is not clear. The great discoverers have had to withstand the herd, and incur hostility by their independence. But the average man's opinions are much less foolish than they would be if he thought for himself: in science, at least, his respect for authority is on the whole beneficial.

I think that in the life of a man whose circumstances and talents are not very exceptional there should be a large sphere where what is vaguely termed "herd instinct" dominates, and a small sphere into which it does not penetrate. The small sphere should contain the region of his special competence. We think ill of a man who cannot admire a woman unless everybody else also admires her: we think that, in the choice of a wife, a man should be guided by his own independent feelings, not by a reflection of the feelings of his society. It is no matter if his judgments of people in general agree with those of his neighbours, but when he falls in love he ought to be guided by his own independent feelings. Much the same thing applies in other directions. A farmer should follow his own judgment as to the capacities of the fields which he cultivates himself, though his judgment should be formed after acquiring a knowledge of scientific agriculture. An economist should form an independent judgment on currency questions, but an ordinary mortal had better follow authority. Wherever there is special competence, there should be independence. But a man should not make himself into a kind of hedgehog, all bristles to keep the world at a distance. The bulk of our ordinary activities must be co-operative, and co-operation must have an instinctive basis. Nevertheless, we should all learn to be able to think for ourselves about matters that are particularly well known to us, and we ought all to have acquired the courage to proclaim unpopular opinions when we believe them to be important. The application of these broad principles in special cases may, of course, be difficult. But it will be less difficult than it is at present in a world where men commonly have the virtues we have been considering in this chapter. The persecuted saint, for instance, would not exist in such a world. The good man would have no occasion to bristle and become self-conscious; his goodness would result from following his impulses, and would be combined with instinctive happiness. His neighbours would not hate him, because they would not fear him: the hatred of pioneers is due to the terror they inspire, and this terror would not exist among men who had acquired courage. Only a man dominated by fear would join the Ku Klux Klan or the Fascisti. In a world of brave men, such persecuting organizations could not exist, and the good life would involve far less resistance to instinct than it does at present. The good world can only be created and sustained by fearless men, but the more they succeed in their task the fewer occasions there will be for the exercise of their courage.

A community of men and women possessing vitality, courage, sensitiveness, and intelligence, in the highest degree that education can produce, would be very different from anything that has hitherto existed. Very few people would be unhappy. The main causes of unhappiness at present are: ill-health, poverty, and an unsatisfactory sex-life. All of these would become very rare. Good health could be almost universal, and even old age could be postponed. Poverty, since the industrial revolution, is only due to collective stupidity. Sensitiveness would make people wish to abolish it, intelligence would show them the way, and courage would lead them to adopt it. (A timid person would rather remain miserable than do anything unusual.) Most people's sex-life, at present, is more or less unsatisfactory. This is partly due to bad education, partly to persecution by the authorities and Mrs. Grundy. A generation of women brought up without irrational sex fears would soon make an end of this. Fear has been thought the only way to make women "virtuous", and they have been deliberately taught to be cowards, both physically and mentally. Women in whom love is cramped encourage brutality and hypocrisy in their husbands, and distort the instincts of their children. One generation of fearless women could transform the world, by bringing into it a generation of fearless children, not contorted into unnatural shapes, but straight and candid, generous, affectionate, and free. Their ardour would sweep away the cruelty and pain which we endure because we are lazy, cowardly, hard-hearted and stupid. It is education that gives us these bad qualities, and education that must give us the opposite virtues. Education is the key to the new world.

But it is time to have done with generalities and come to the concrete detail in which our ideals are to be embodied.

PART II
EDUCATION OF CHARACTER

CHAPTER III

THE FIRST YEAR

THE first year of life was formerly regarded as lying outside the sphere of education. At least until the infant could speak, if not longer, it was left to the entirely unchecked care of mothers and nurses, who were supposed to know by instinct what was good for the child. As a matter of fact, they did not know. An enormous proportion of children died during the first year, and of the remainder many were already ruined in health. By bad handling, the foundations had been laid for disastrous habits of mind. All this has only recently been realized. The invasion of the nursery by science is often resented, because it disturbs the sentimental picture of mother and child. But sentimentality and love cannot coexist; the parent who loves his or her child will wish it to live, even if it should be necessary to employ intelligence for the purpose. Accordingly we find this sentimentality strongest in childless people and in people who, like Rousseau, are willing to leave their children to the Foundling

Hospital. Most educated parents are eager to know what science has to say, and uneducated parents, also, learn from maternity centres. The result is shown in the remarkable diminution of infant mortality. There is reason to think that, with adequate care and skill, very few children would die in infancy. Not only would few die, but the survivors would be healthier in mind and body.

Questions of physical health, strictly speaking, lie outside the scope of this book, and must be left to medical practitioners. I shall touch on them only where they have psychological importance. But physical and mental are scarcely distinguishable in the first year of life. Moreover the educator in later years may find himself handicapped by purely physiological mistakes in handling the infant. We cannot therefore altogether avoid trespassing upon ground which does not of right belong to us.

The new-born infant has reflexes and instincts, but no habits. Whatever habits it may have acquired in the womb are useless in its new situation: even breathing sometimes has to be taught, and some children die because they do not learn the lesson quickly enough. There is one well-developed instinct, the instinct of sucking; when the child is engaged in this occupation, it feels at home with its new environment. But the rest of its waking life is

passed in a vague bewilderment, from which
relief is found by sleeping most of the twenty-
four hours. At the end of a fortnight, all this
is changed. The child has acquired expectations from regularly recurring experiences.
It is already a conservative—probably a more
complete conservative than at any later time.
Any novelty is met with resentment. If it
could speak, it would say: "Do you suppose I
am going to change the habits of a lifetime at
my time of life?" The rapidity with which
infants acquire habits is amazing. Every bad
habit acquired is a barrier to better habits later;
that is why the first formation of habits in early
infancy is so important. If the first habits are
good, endless trouble is saved later. Moreover
habits acquired very early feel, in later life,
just like instincts; they have the same profound
grip. New contrary habits acquired afterwards cannot have the same force; for this
reason, also, the first habits should be a matter
of grave concern.

Two considerations come in when we are
considering habit-formation in infancy. The
first and paramount consideration is health; the
second is character. We want the child to
become the sort of person that will be liked and
will be able to cope with life successfully.
Fortunately, health and character point in the
same direction: what is good for one is good also

for the other. It is character that specially concerns us in this book; but health requires the same practices. Thus we are not faced with the difficult alternative of a healthy scoundrel or a diseased saint.

Every educated mother nowadays knows such simple facts as the importance of feeding the infant at regular intervals, not whenever it cries. This practice has arisen because it is better for the child's digestion, which is an entirely sufficient reason. But it is also desirable from the point of view of moral education. Infants are far more cunning than grown-up people are apt to suppose; if they find that crying produces agreeable results, they will cry. When, in later life, a habit of complaining causes them to be disliked instead of petted, they feel surprised and resentful, and the world seems to them cold and unsympathetic. If, however, they grow up into charming women, they will still be petted when they are querulous, and the bad training begun in childhood will be intensified. The same thing is true of rich men. Unless the right methods are adopted in infancy, people in later life will be either discontented or grasping, according to the degree of their power. The right moment to begin the requisite moral training is the moment of birth, because then it can be begun without disappointing expectations. At any later time it will have to fight against contrary habits, and will therefore be met by resentful indignation.

In dealing with the infant, therefore, there is need of a delicate balance between neglect and indulgence. Everything necessary for health must be done. The child must be picked up when it suffers from wind, it must be kept dry and warm. But if it cries when there is no adequate physical cause, it must be left to cry; if not, it will quickly develop into a tyrant. When it is attended to, there should not be too much fuss: what is necessary must be done, but without excessive expressions of sympathy. At no period of its life must it be regarded as an agreeable pet, somewhat more interesting than a lap-dog. It must from the very first be viewed seriously, as a potential adult. Habits which would be intolerable in an adult may be quite pleasant in a child. Of course the child cannot actually have the habits of an adult, but we should avoid everything that places an obstacle in the way of the acquisition of these habits. Above all, we should not give the child a sense of self-importance which later experience will mortify, and which, in any case, is not in accordance with the facts.

The difficulty in the education of young infants is largely the delicate balance required in the parent. Constant watchfulness and much labour are needed to avoid injury to health; these qualities will hardly exist in the necessary degree except where there is strong parental affection. But where this exists, it is very likely not to be wise. To the devoted parent, the child is immensely important. Unless care is taken, the child feels this, and judges himself as important as his parents feel him. In later life, his social environment will not regard him so fondly, and habits which assume that he is the centre of other people's universe will lead to disappointment. It is therefore necessary, not only in the first year, but afterwards also, that the parents should be breezy and cheerful and rather matter-of-fact where the child's possible ailments are concerned. In old days, infants were at once restricted and coddled: their limbs were not free, they were too warmly dressed, they were hampered in their spontaneous activities, but they were petted, sung to, rocked and dandled. This was ideally wrong, since it turned them into helpless pampered parasites.[1] The right rule is: encourage spontaneous activities, but discourage demands upon others. Do not let the child see how much you do for it, or how much trouble you take. Let it, wherever possible, taste the joy of a success achieved by its own efforts, not

[1] If it be objected that, after all, the world progressed, the reply is that it did not progress nearly as fast as it might have done, or as it will do if children are wisely handled.

extracted by tyrannizing over the grown-ups. Our aim, in modern education, is to reduce external discipline to a minimum; but this requires an internal self-discipline which is much more easily acquired in the first year of life than at any other time. For example: when you want a child to sleep, do not wheel it up and down, or take it in your arms, or even stay where it can see you. If you do this once, the child will demand that you should do it next time; in an incredibly short space of time it becomes a terrific business to get the child to sleep. Make it warm and dry and comfortable, put it down firmly, and after a few quiet remarks leave it to itself. It may cry for a few minutes, but unless it is ill it will soon stop. If you then go to look, you will find that it is fast asleep. And it will sleep far more with this treatment than with petting and indulgence.

The new-born infant, as we observed before, has no habits, but only reflexes and instincts. It follows that his world is not composed of "objects". Recurrent experiences are necessary for recognition, and recognition is necessary before the conception of an "object" can arise. The feel of the cot, the feel and smell of the mother's breast (or the bottle), and the mother's or nurse's voice will soon come to be familiar. The visual appearance of the mother or the cot comes somewhat later, because the new-born child does not know how to focus so as to see shapes distinctly. It is only gradually, through the formation of habits by association, that touch and sight and smell and hearing come together and coalesce in the common-sense notion of an object, of which one manifestation leads to the expectation of another. Even then, for a time, there is hardly any feeling of the difference between persons and things; a baby which is partly breast-fed and partly bottle-fed will, for a time, have similar feelings towards mother and bottle. During all this time, education must be by purely physical means. Its pleasures are physical—chiefly food and warmth—and its pains also are physical. Habits of behaviour arise through seeking what is associated with pleasure and avoiding what is associated with pain. A child's crying is partly a reflex connected with pain, partly an act performed in the pursuit of pleasure. At first, of course, it is only the former. But since any real pain that the child may be suffering must, if possible, be removed, it is inevitable that crying should come to be associated with pleasant consequences. The child therefore soon begins to cry because it desires a pleasure, not because it feels a physical pain; this is one of its first triumphs of intelligence. But try as it may, it cannot give quite the same cry as when it is in actual pain. The attentive ear of the mother knows the difference, and if she is wise she will ignore the cry that is not an expression of physical pain. It is easy and agreeable to amuse an infant by dandling it or singing to it. But it learns with amazing rapidity to demand more and more of such amusements, which soon interfere with necessary sleep—and sleep ought to occupy almost all the day except meal-times. Some of these precepts may seem harsh, but experience shows that they make for the child's health and happiness.

But while the amusements which grown-up people provide should be kept within certain limits, those which the infant can enjoy for itself should be encouraged to the utmost. From the first, it should have opportunities to kick and practise its muscles. How our ancestors can have so long persisted in the practice of swaddling-clothes is almost inconceivable; it shows that even parental affection has difficulty in overcoming laziness, since the infant whose limbs are free needs more attention. As soon as the child can focus, it finds pleasure in watching moving objects, especially things that wave in the wind. But the number of possible amusements is small until the child has learned to grasp objects that it sees. Then, immediately, there is an enormous accession of pleasure. For some time, the exercise of grasping is enough to secure the happiness of many waking hours. Pleasure in a rattle also comes at this stage. Slightly earlier is the conquest of the toes and fingers. At first, the movement of the toes is purely reflex; then the baby discovers that they can be moved at will. This gives all the pleasure of an imperialist conquering a foreign country: the toes cease to be alien bodies and become incorporated in the ego. From this time onward, the child should be able to find many amusements, provided suitable objects are within his reach. And a child's amusements, for the most part, will be just what its education requires—provided, of course that it is not allowed to tumble, or to swallow pins, or otherwise injure itself.

The first three months of life are, on the whole, a somewhat dreary time for the infant, except during the moments when it is enjoying its meals. When it is comfortable, it sleeps; when it is awake, there is usually some discomfort. The happiness of a human being depends upon mental capacities, but these can find little outlet in an infant under three months, for lack of experience and muscular control. Young animals enjoy life much sooner, because they depend more upon instinct and less upon experience; but the things an infant can do by instinct are too few to provide more than a minimum of pleasure and interest. On the whole, the first three months involve a good deal of boredom. But the boredom is necessary if there is to be enough sleep; if much is done to amuse the child, it will not sleep enough.

At about the age of two to three months, the child learns to smile, and to have feelings about persons which are different from its feelings about things. At this age, a social relation between mother and child begins to be possible: the child can and does show pleasure at the sight of the mother, and develops responses which are not merely animal. Very soon a desire for praise and approval grows up; in my own boy, it was first shown unmistakably at the age of five months, when he succeeded, after many attempts, in lifting a somewhat heavy bell off the table, and ringing it while he looked round at everybody with a proud smile. From this moment, the educator has a new weapon: praise and blame. This weapon is extraordinarily powerful throughout childhood, but it must be used with great caution. There should not be any blame at all during the first year, and afterwards it should be used very sparingly. Praise is less harmful. But it should not be given so easily as to lose its value, nor should it be used to overstimulate a child. No tolerable parent could refrain from praising a child when it first walks and when it first says an intelligible word. And generally, when a child has mastered a difficulty after persistent efforts, praise is a proper reward. Moreover it is well to let the child feel that you sympathize with his desire to learn.

But on the whole an infant's desire to learn is so strong that parents need only provide opportunity. Give the child a chance to develop, and his own efforts will do the rest. It is not necessary to teach a child to crawl, or to walk, or to learn any of the other elements of muscular control. Of course we teach a child to talk by talking to it, but I doubt whether any purpose is served by deliberate attempts to teach words. Children learn at their own pace, and it is a mistake to try to force them. The great incentive to effort, all through life, is experience of success after initial difficulties. The difficulties must not be so great as to cause discouragement, or so small as not to stimulate effort. From birth to death, this is a fundamental principle. It is by what we do ourselves that we learn. What grown-up people can do is to perform some simple action that the child would like to perform, such as rattling a rattle, and then let the child find out how to do it. What others do is merely a stimulus to ambition; it is never in itself an education.

Regularity and routine are of the utmost importance in early childhood, and most of all in the first year of life. In regard to sleep, food, and evacuation, regular habits should be formed from the start. Moreover familiarity of surroundings is very important mentally. It teaches recognition, it avoids overstrain, and it produces a feeling of safety. I have sometimes thought that belief in the uniformity of nature, which is said to be a postulate of science, is entirely derived from the wish for safety. We can cope with the expected, but if the laws of nature were suddenly changed we should perish. The infant, because of its weakness, has need of reassurance, and it will be happier if everything that happens seems to happen according to invariable laws, so as to be predictable. In later childhood, the love of adventure develops, but in the first year of life everything unusual tends to be alarming. Do not let the child feel fear if you can possibly help it. If it is ill, and you are anxious, hide your anxiety very carefully, lest it should pass to the child by suggestion. Avoid everything that might produce excitement. And do not minister to the child's self-importance by letting it see that you mind if it does not sleep or eat or evacuate as it should. This applies not only to the first year of life, but still more to the subsequent years. Never let the child think that a necessary normal action, such as eating which ought to be a pleasure, is something that you desire, and that you want it to do so to please you. If you do, the child soon perceives that it has acquired a new source of power, and expects to be coaxed into actions which it ought to perform spontaneously. Do not imagine that the child has not the intelligence for such behaviour. Its powers are small and its knowledge is limited, but it has just as much intelligence as a grown-up person where these limitations do not operate. It learns more in the first twelve months than it will ever learn again in the same space of time, and this would be impossible if it had not a very active intelligence.

To sum up: Treat even the youngest baby with respect, as a person who will have to take his place in the world. Do not sacrifice his future to your present convenience, or to your pleasure in making much of him: the one is as harmful as the other. Here, as elsewhere, a combination of love and knowledge is necessary if the right way is to be followed.

CHAPTER IV

FEAR

In the following chapters, I propose to deal
with various aspects of moral education, especially in the years from the second to the sixth.
By the time the child is six years old, moral
education ought to be nearly complete; that is
to say, the further virtues which will be required in later years ought to be developed by
the boy or girl spontaneously, as a result of good
habits already existing and ambitions already
stimulated. It is only where early moral training has been neglected or badly given that
much will be needed at later ages.

I suppose that the child has reached the age
of twelve months healthy and happy, with the
foundations of a disciplined character already
well laid by the methods considered in the preceding chapter. There will, of course, be some
children whose health is bad, even if parents
take all the precautions known to science at
present. But we may hope that their number
will be enormously diminished as time goes on.
They ought, even now, to be so few as to be
statistically unimportant, if existing knowledge

were adequately applied. I do not propose to consider what ought to be done with children whose early training has been bad. This is a problem for the school-master, not for the parent; and it is especially to the parent that this book is addressed.

The second year of life should be one of great happiness. Walking and talking are new accomplishments, bringing a sense of freedom and power. Every day the child improves in both.[1] Independent play becomes possible, and the child has a more vivid sense of "seeing the world" than a man can derive from the most extensive globe-trotting. Birds and flowers, rivers and the sea, motor-cars and trains and steamers all bring delight and passionate interest. Curiosity is boundless: "want to see" is one of the commonest phrases at this age. Running freely in a garden or a field or on the seashore produces an ecstasy of emancipation after the confinement of crib and baby-carriage. Digestion is usually stronger than in the first year, food is more varied, and mastication is a new joy. For all these reasons, if the child is well cared for and healthy, life is a delicious adventure.

But with the greater independence of walk-

---

[1] This is perhaps not strictly accurate. Most children have periods of apparent stagnation, which cause anxiety to inexperienced parents. But probably throughout these periods there is progress in ways that are not easily perceptible.

ing and running there is apt to come also a new timidity. The new-born infant can easily be frightened; Dr. J. B. and Mrs. Watson found that the things which alarm it most are loud noises and the sensation of being dropped.[2] It is, however, so completely protected that it has little occasion for the rational exercise of fear; even in real dangers it is helpless, so that fear would not be of any use to it. During the second and third year, new fears develop. It is a moot point how far this is due to suggestion, and how far it is instinctive. The fact that the fears do not exist during the first year is not conclusive against their instinctive character, since an instinct may ripen at any age. Not even the most extreme Freudian would maintain that the sex-instinct is mature at birth. Obviously children who can run about by themselves have more need of fear than infants that cannot walk; it would therefore not be surprising if the instinct of fear arose with the need. The question is of considerable educational importance. If all fears arise from suggestion, they can be prevented by the simple expedient of not showing fear or aversion before a child. If, on the other hand, some of them are instinctive, more elaborate methods will be required.

Dr. Chalmers Mitchell, in his book "The

[2] "Studies in Infant Psychology", *Scientific Monthly*, December, 1921, p. 506.

Childhood of Animals", gives a large number of observations and experiments to show that there is usually no inherited instinct of fear in young animals.[3] Except monkeys and a few birds, they view the age-long enemies of their species, such as snakes, without the slightest alarm, unless their parents have taught them to feel fear of these animals. Children well under a year old seem never to be afraid of animals. Dr. Watson taught one such child to be afraid of rats by repeatedly sounding a gong behind its head at the moment when he showed it a rat. The noise was terrifying, and the rat came to be so by association. But instinctive fear of animals seems quite unknown in the early months. Fear of the dark, also, seems never to occur in children who have not been exposed to the suggestion that the dark is terrifying. There are certainly very strong grounds for the view that most of the fears which we used to regard as instinctive are acquired, and would not arise if grown-up people did not create them.

In order to get fresh light on this subject, I have observed my own children carefully; but as I could not always know what nurses and maids might have said to them, the interpretation of the facts was often doubtful. So far

[3] I came to know of these passages from a quotation in Dr. Paul Bousfield's "Sex and Civilization", where the same point of view is strongly advocated.

as I could judge, they bore out Dr. Watson's views as to fear in the first year of life. In the second year, they showed no fear of animals, except that one of them, for a time, was afraid of horses. This, however, was apparently due to the fact that a horse had suddenly galloped past her with a very loud noise. She is still in her second year, and therefore for later observation I am dependent on the boy. Near the end of his second year, he had a new nurse who was generally timid and especially afraid of the dark. He quickly acquired her terrors (of which we were ignorant at first); he fled from dogs and cats, cowered in abject fear before a dark cupboard, wanted lights in every part of the room after dark, and was even afraid of his little sister the first time he saw her, thinking, apparently, that she was a strange animal of some unknown species.[4] All these fears might have been acquired from the timid nurse; in fact they gradually faded away after she was gone. There were other fears, however, which could not be accounted for in the same way, since they began before the nurse came, and were directed to objects which no grown-up person would find alarming. Chief of these was a fear of everything that moved in a surprising way, notably shadows and mechanical

[4] I think this fear was the same as the fear of mechanical toys. He saw her first asleep, and thought she was a doll; when she moved he was startled.

toys. After making this observation, I learned
that fears of this sort are normal in childhood,
and that there are strong reasons for regarding
them as instinctive. The matter is discussed
by William Stern in his "Psychology of Early
Childhood", p. 494 ff, under the heading "Fear
of the Mysterious". What he says is as follows:

The special significance of this form of fear, particularly in early childhood, has escaped the notice of
the older school of child-psychologists; it has lately
been established by Groos and by us. "Fear of the
unaccustomed seems to be more a part of primitive
nature than fear of a known danger" (Groos, p. 284).
If the child meets with anything that does not fit in
with the familiar course of his perception, three
things are possible. Either the impression is so alien
that it is simply rejected as a foreign body, and consciousness takes no notice of it. Or the interruption
of the usual course of perception is pronounced
enough to attract attention but not so violent as to
effect disturbance; it is rather surprise, desire for
knowledge, the beginning of all thought, judgment,
enquiry. Or, lastly, the new suddenly breaks in
upon the old with violent intensity, throws familiar
ideas into unexpected confusion without a possibility
of an immediate practical adjustment; then follows
a shock with a strong affective-tone of displeasure,
the fear of the mysterious (uncanny). Groos now
has pointed out with keen insight that this fear of
the uncanny is also distinctly founded on instinctive
fear; it corresponds to a biological necessity which
works from one generation to the next.

Stern gives many instances, among others fear of a suddenly opened umbrella and "the frequent fear of mechanical toys". The former, by the way, is very strong in horses and cows: a large herd can be driven into headlong flight by it, as I have verified. My own boy's terrors, under this head, were just such as Stern describes. The shadows that frightened him were vague quickly-moving shadows thrown into a room by unseen objects (such as omnibuses) passing in the street. I cured him by making shadows on the wall and the floor with my fingers, and getting him to imitate me; before long, he felt that he understood shadows and began to enjoy them. The same principle applied to mechanical toys: when he had seen the mechanism he was no longer frightened. But when the mechanism was invisible the process was slow. Some one gave him a cushion which emitted a long melancholy whine after being sat upon or pressed. This alarmed him for a long time. In no case did we entirely remove the terrifying object: we put it at a distance, where it was only slightly alarming; we produced gradual familiarity; and we persisted till the fear completely ceased. Generally the same mysterious quality which caused fear at first produced delight when the fear had been overcome. I think an irrational fear should never be simply let alone, but should be gradually overcome by familiarity with its fainter forms.

We adopted an exactly opposite process—perhaps wrongly—in the case of two rational fears which were wholly absent. I live half the year on a rocky coast where there are many precipices. The boy had no sense whatever of the danger of heights, and would have run straight over a cliff into the sea if we had let him. One day when we were sitting on a steep slope that ended in a sheer drop of a hundred feet, we explained to him quietly, as a merely scientific fact, that if he went over the edge he would fall and break like a plate. (He had lately seen a plate broken into many pieces by being dropped on the floor.) He sat still for some time, saying to himself "fall", "break", and then asked to be taken further from the edge. This was at the age of about two and a half. Since then he has had just enough fear of heights to make him safe while we keep an eye on him. But he would still be very rash if left to himself. He now (three and nine months) jumps from heights of six feet without hesitation, and would jump twenty feet if we would let him. Thus the instruction in apprehension certainly did not produce excessive results. I attribute this to the fact that it was instruction, not suggestion; neither of us was feeling fear when the instruction was given. I regard this as very important in education. Rational apprehension of dangers is necessary; fear is not. A child cannot apprehend dangers without *some* element of fear, but this element is very much diminished when it is not present in the instructor. A grown-up person in charge of a child should never feel fear. That is one reason why courage should be cultivated in women just as much as in men.

The second illustration was less deliberate. One day when I was walking with the boy (at the age of three years and four months) we found an adder on the path. He had seen pictures of snakes, but had never before seen a real snake. He did not know that snakes bite. He was delighted with the adder, and when it glided away he ran after it. As I knew he could not catch it, I did not check him, and did not tell him that snakes are dangerous. His nurse, however, from that time on, prevented him from running in long grass, on the ground that there might be snakes. A slight fear grew up in him as a result, but not more than we felt to be desirable.

The most difficult fear to overcome, so far, has been fear of the sea. Our first attempt to take the boy into the sea was at the age of two and a half. At first, it was quite impossible. He disliked the cold of the water, he was frightened by the noise of the waves, and they seemed to him to be always coming, never going. If the waves were big, he would not even go near to the sea. This was a period of general timidity; animals, odd noises, and various other things, caused alarm. We dealt with fear of the sea piecemeal. We put the boy into shallow pools away from the sea, until the mere cold had ceased to be a shock; at the end of the four warm months, he enjoyed paddling in shallow water at a distance from waves, but still cried if we put him into deep pools where the water came up to his waist. We accustomed him to the noise of the waves by letting him play for an hour at a time just out of sight of them; then we took him to where he could see them, and made him notice that after coming in they go out again. All this, combined with the example of his parents and other children, only brought him to the point where he could be *near* the waves without fear. I am convinced that the fear was instinctive; I am fairly certain there had **been** no suggestion to cause it. The following summer, at the age of three and a half, **we** took the matter up again. There was still **a** terror of going actually into the waves. After some unsuccessful coaxing, combined with the spectacle of everybody else bathing, we adopted old-fashioned methods. When he showed cowardice, we made him feel that we were ashamed of him; when he showed courage, we praised him warmly. Every day for about a fortnight, we plunged him up to the neck in the sea, in spite of his struggles and cries.[5] Every day they grew less; before they ceased, he began to ask to be put in. At the end of a fortnight, the desired result had been achieved: he no longer feared the sea. From that moment, we left him completely free, and he bathed of his own accord whenever the weather was suitable —obviously with the greatest enjoyment. Fear had not ceased altogether, but had been partly repressed by pride. Familiarity, however, made the fear grow rapidly less, and it has now ceased altogether. His sister, now twenty months old, has never shown any fear of the sea, and runs straight in without the slightest hesitation.

I have related this matter in some detail, be-cause, to a certain extent, it goes against modern theories for which I have much respect. The use of force in education should be very rare. But for the conquest of fear it is, I think, some-times salutary. Where a fear is irrational and strong, the child, left to himself, will never have the experiences which show that there is no ground for apprehension. When a situation has been experienced repeatedly without harm,

---

[5] The method adopted with me at the same age was to pick me up by the heels and hold my head under water for some time. This method, oddly enough, succeeded in making me like the water; nevertheless I do not recommend it.

familiarity kills fear.   It would very likely be useless to give the dreaded experience *once*; it must be given often enough to become in no degree surprising.   If the necessary experience can be secured without force, so much the better; but if not, force may be better than the persistence of an unconquered fear.

There is a further point.   In the case of my own boy, and presumably in other cases too, the experience of overcoming fear is extraordinarily delightful.   It is easy to rouse the boy's pride: when he has won praise for courage, he is radiantly happy for the rest of the day. At a later stage, a timid boy suffers agonies through the contempt of other boys, and it is much more difficult then for him to acquire new habits.   I think therefore that the early acquisition of self-control in the matter of fear, and the early teaching of physical enterprise, are of sufficient importance to warrant somewhat drastic methods.

Parents learn by their mistakes; it is only when the children are grown up that one discovers how they ought to have been educated. I shall therefore relate an incident which shows the snares of overindulgence.   At the age of two and a half, my boy was put to sleep in a room by himself.   He was inordinately proud of the promotion from the night-nursery, and at first he always slept quietly through the night. But one night there was a terrific gale, and a hurdle was blown over with a deafening crash. He woke in terror, and cried out. I went to him at once: he had apparently waked with a nightmare, and clung to me with his heart beating wildly. Very soon his terror ceased. But he had complained that it was dark—usually, at that time of year, he slept all through the dark hours. After I left him, the terror seemed to return in a mitigated form, so I gave him a night-light. After that, he made an almost nightly practice of crying out, until at last it became clear that he was only doing it for the pleasure of having grown-up people come and make a fuss. So we talked to him very carefully about the absence of danger in the dark, and told him that if he woke he was to turn over and go to sleep again, as we should not come to him unless there was something serious the matter. He listened attentively, and never cried out again except for grave cause on rare occasions. Of course the night-light was discontinued. If we had been more indulgent, we should probably have made him sleep badly for a long time, perhaps for life.

So much from personal experience. We must now pass on to a more general consideration of methods for eliminating fear.

After the first years, the proper instructors in

physical courage are other children.   If a child
has older brothers and sisters, they will stimulate it both by example and by precept, and
whatever they can do it will attempt.   At
school, physical cowardice is despised, and there
is no need for grown-up teachers to emphasize
the matter.   At least, that is the case among
boys.   It ought to be equally the case among
girls, who should have precisely the same
standards of courage.   In physical ways, fortunately, school-girls are no longer taught to be
"lady-like", and their natural impulses towards
physical prowess are allowed a fair amount of
scope.   There is still, however, some difference
between boys and girls in this respect.   I am
convinced there ought to be none.[6]

   When I speak of courage as desirable, I am
taking a purely behaviorist definition: a man
is courageous when he does things which others
might fail to do owing to fear.   If he feels no
fear, so much the better; I do not regard control
of fear by the will as the only true courage, or
even as the best form of courage.   The secret
of modern moral education is to produce results by means of good habits which were formerly produced (or attempted) by self-control
and will-power.   Courage due to the will produces nervous disorders, of which "shell-
shock" afforded numerous instances.   The fears

[6] See Bousfield, "Sex and Civilization", *passim.*

which had been repressed forced their way to
the surface in ways not recognizable to intro-
spection. I do not mean to suggest that self-
control can be dispensed with entirely; on the
contrary, no man can live a consistent life without it. What I do mean is, that self-control
ought only to be needed in unforeseen situations,
for which education has not provided in advance. It would have been foolish, even if it
had been possible, to train the whole population
to have, without effort, the sort of courage that
was needed in the war. This was an exceptional
and temporary need, of so extraordinary a kind
that all other education would have had to be
stunted if the habits required in the trenches
had been instilled in youth.

The late Dr. Rivers, in his book on "Instinct
and the Unconscious", gives the best psychological analysis of fear with which I am
acquainted. He points out that one way of
meeting a dangerous situation is manipulative
activity, and that those who are able to employ this method adequately do not, at least
consciously, feel the emotion of fear. It is a
valuable experience, which stimulates both self-
respect and effort, to pass gradually from fear
to skill. Even so simple a matter as learning
to ride a bicycle will give this experience in a
mild form. In the modern world, owing to in-

crease of mechanism, this sort of skill is becoming more and more important.

I suggest that training in physical courage should be as far as possible given by teaching skill in manipulating or controlling matter, not by means of bodily contests with other human beings. The kind of courage required for mountaineering, for manipulating an aeroplane, or for managing a small ship in a gale, seems to me far more admirable than the sort required in fighting. As far as possible, therefore, I should train school-children in forms of more or less dangerous dexterity, rather than in such things as football. Where there is an enemy to be overcome, let it be matter rather than other human beings. I do not mean that this principle should be applied pedantically, but that it should be allowed more weight in athletics than is the case at present.

There are, of course, more passive aspects of physical courage. There is endurance of hurts without making a fuss; this can be taught to children by not giving too much sympathy when they have small mishaps. A great deal of hysteria in later life consists mainly of an excessive desire for sympathy: people invent ailments in the hope of being petted and treated softly. This disposition can usually be prevented from developing by not encouraging children to cry over every scratch and bruise.

In this respect, the education of the nursery is still much worse for girls than for boys. It is just as bad to be soft with girls as with boys; if women are to be the equals of men, they must not be inferior in the sterner virtues.

I come now to the forms of courage that are not purely physical. These are the more important forms, but it is difficult to develop them adequately except on a foundation of the more elementary kinds.

The fear of the mysterious has been already touched upon, in connection with childish terrors. I believe this fear to be instinctive, and of immense historical importance. Most superstition is due to it. Eclipses, earthquakes, plagues, and such occurrences arouse it in a high degree among unscientific populations. It is a very dangerous form of fear, both individually and socially; to eradicate it in youth is therefore highly desirable. The proper antidote to it is scientific explanation. It is not necessary that everything which is mysterious at first sight should be explained: after a certain number of explanations have been given, the child will assume that there are explanations in other cases, and it will become possible to say that the explanation cannot be given yet. The important thing is to produce, as soon as possible, the feeling that the sense of mystery is only due to ignorance, which can be dispelled

by patience and mental effort.   It is a remarkable fact that the very things which terrify
children at first by their mysterious properties
delight them as soon as fear is overcome.   Thus
mystery becomes an incentive to study, as soon
as it ceases to promote superstition.   My little
boy, at the age of three and a half, spent many
hours in absorbed solitary study of a garden
syringe, until he had grasped how the water
came in and the air came out, and how the
converse process occurred.   Eclipses can be explained so as to be intelligible even to very tiny
children.   Whatever either terrifies or interests
the child should be explained if it is at all
possible; this transforms fear into scientific interest by a process which is entirely along the
lines of instinct and repeats the history of the
race.

Some problems, in this connection, are difficult, and require much tact.   The most difficult
is death.   The child soon discovers that plants
and animals die.   The chances are that some-
body he knows will die before he is six years
old.   If he has at all an active mind, it occurs
to him that his parents will die, and even that he
will die himself.   (This is more difficult to
imagine.)   These thoughts will produce a crop
of questions, which must be answered carefully.
A person whose beliefs are orthodox will have
less difficulty than a person who thinks that

there is no life after death. If you hold the latter view, do not say anything contrary to it; no consideration on earth justifies a parent in telling lies to his child. It is best to explain that death is a sleep from which people do not wake. This should be said without solemnity, as if it were the most ordinary thing imaginable. If the child worries about dying himself, tell him it is not likely to happen for many, many years. It would be useless, in early years, to attempt to instil a Stoic contempt for death. Do not introduce the topic, but do not avoid it when the child introduces it. Do all you can to make the child feel that there is no mystery about it. If he is a normal healthy child, these methods will suffice to keep him from brooding. At all ages, be willing to talk fully and frankly, to tell all that you believe, and to convey the impression that the subject is rather uninteresting. It is not good either for old or young to spend much time in thinking about death.

Apart from special fears, children are liable to a diffused anxiety. This is generally due to too much repression by their elders, and is therefore much less common than it used to be. Perpetual nagging, prohibition of noise, constant instruction in manners, used to make childhood a period of misery. I can remember, at the age of five, being told that childhood was the happiest period of life (a blank lie, in those days). I wept inconsolably, wished I were dead, and wondered how I should endure the boredom of the years to come. It is almost inconceivable, nowadays, that any one should say such a thing to a child. The child's life is instinctively prospective: it is always directed towards the things that will become possible later on. This is part of the stimulus to the child's efforts. To make the child retrospective, to represent the future as worse than the past, is to sap the life of the child at its source. Yet that is what heartless sentimentalists used to do by talking to the child about the joys of childhood. Fortunately the impression of their words did not last long. At most times, I believed the grown-ups must be perfectly happy, because they had no lessons and they could eat what they liked. This belief was healthy and stimulating.

Shyness is a distressing form of timidity, which is common in England and China, and parts of America, but rare elsewhere. It arises partly from having little to do with strangers, partly from insistence upon company manners. As far as is convenient, children should, after the first year, become accustomed to seeing strangers and being handled by them. As regards manners, they should, at first, be taught the bare minimum required for not being an intolerable nuisance.

It is better to let them see strangers for a few minutes without restraint and then be taken away, than to expect them to stay in the room and be quiet. But after the first two years it is a good plan to teach them to amuse themselves quietly part of the day, with pictures or clay or Montessori apparatus or something of the kind. There should always be a reason for quiet that they can understand. Manners should not be taught in the abstract, except when it can be done as an amusing game. But as soon as the child can understand he should realize that parents also have their rights; he must accord freedom to others, and have freedom for himself to the utmost possible extent. Children easily appreciate justice, and will readily accord to others what others accord to them. This is the core of good manners.

Above all, if you wish to dispel fear in your children, be fearless yourself. If you are afraid of thunderstorms, the child will catch your fear the first time he hears thunder in your presence. If you express a dread of social revolution, the child will feel a fright all the greater for not knowing what you are talking about. If you are apprehensive about illness, so will your child be. Life is full of perils, but the wise man ignores those that are inevitable, and acts prudently but without emotion as regards those that can be avoided. You cannot avoid dying, but you can avoid dying intestate; therefore make your will, and forget that you are mortal. Rational provision against misfortune is a totally different thing from fear; it is a part of wisdom, whereas all fear is slavish. If you cannot avoid feeling fears, try to prevent your child from suspecting them. Above all, give him that wide outlook and that multiplicity of vivid interests that will prevent him, in later life, from brooding upon possibilities of personal misfortune. Only so can you make him a free citizen of the universe.

CHAPTER V

LOVE of play is the most obvious distinguish-
ing mark of young animals, whether human or
otherwise. In human children, this is accom-
panied by an inexhaustible pleasure in pretence.
Play and pretence are a vital need of childhood,
for which opportunity must be provided if the
child is to be happy and healthy, quite inde-
pendently of any further utility in these activities. There are two questions which concern
education in this connection: first, what should
parents and schools do in the way of providing
opportunity? and secondly, should they do anything more, with a view to increasing the
educational usefulness of games?

Let us begin with a few words about the
psychology of games. This has been exhaus-
tively treated by Groos; a shorter discussion
will be found in William Stern's book mentioned in the preceding chapter. There are
two separate questions in this matter: the first
is as to the impulses which produce play, the
second is as to its biological utility. The second

is the easier question. There seems no reason to doubt the most widely accepted theory, that in play the young of any species rehearse and practise the activities which they will have to perform in earnest later on. The play of puppies is exactly like a dog-fight, except that they do not actually bite each other. The play of kittens resembles the behaviour of cats with mice. Children love to imitate any work they have been watching, such as building or digging; the more important the work seems to them, the more they like to play at it. And they enjoy anything that gives them new muscular facilities, such as jumping, climbing, or walking up a narrow plank—always provided the task is not too difficult. But although this accounts, in a general way, for the usefulness of the play-impulse, it does not by any means cover all its manifestations, and must not for a moment be regarded as giving a psychological analysis.

Some psycho-analysts have tried to see a sexual symbolism in children's play. This, I am convinced, is utter moonshine. The main instinctive urge of childhood is not sex, but the desire to become adult, or, perhaps more correctly, the will to power.[1] The child is impressed by his own weakness in comparison with

---

[1] Cf. "The Nervous Child" by Dr. H. C. Cameron (3rd ed., Oxford, 1924), p. 32 ff.

older people, and he wishes to become their equal. I remember my boy's profound delight when he realized that he would one day be a man and that I had once been a child; one could see effort being stimulated by the realization that success was possible. From a very early age, the child wishes to do what older people do, as is shown by the practice of imitation. Older brothers and sisters are useful, because their purposes can be understood and their capacities are not so far out of reach as those of grown-up people. The feeling of inferiority is very strong in children; when they are normal and rightly educated, it is a stimulus to effort, but if they are repressed it may become a source of unhappiness.

In play, we have two forms of the will to power: the form which consists in learning to do things, and the form which consists in fantasy. Just as the balked adult may indulge in daydreams that have a sexual significance, so the normal child indulges in pretences that have a power-significance. He likes to be a giant, or a lion, or a train; in his make-believe, he inspires terror. When I told my boy the story of Jack the Giant-Killer, I tried to make him identify himself with Jack, but he firmly chose the giant. When his mother told him the story of Bluebeard, he insisted on being Bluebeard, and regarded the wife as justly punished for in-

subordination. In his play, there was a san-
guinary outbreak of cutting off ladies' heads.
Sadism, Freudians would say; but he enjoyed
just as much being a giant who ate little boys,
or an engine that could pull a heavy load.
Power, not sex, was the common element in
these pretences. One day, when we were re-
turning from a walk, I told him, as an obvious
joke, that perhaps we should find a certain
Mr. Tiddliewinks in possession of our house,
and he might refuse to let us in. After that,
for a long time, he would stand on the porch
being Mr. Tiddliewinks, and telling me to go
to another house. His delight in this game
was unbounded, and obviously the pretence of
power was what he enjoyed.

It would, however, be an undue simplification to suppose that the will to power is the sole
source of children's play. They enjoy the pretence of terror—perhaps because the knowledge
that it is a pretence increases their sense of
safety. Sometimes I pretend to be a crocodile
coming to eat my boy up. He squeals so real-
istically that I stop, thinking he is really
frightened; but the moment I stop he says,
"Daddy be a crocodile again". A good deal of
the pleasure of pretence is sheer joy in drama—
the same thing that makes adults like novels and
the theatre. I think curiosity has a part in all
this: by playing bears, the child feels as if he

were getting to know about bears. I think every strong impulse in the child's life is reflected in play: power is only dominant in his play in proportion as it is dominant in his desires.

As regards the educational value of play, everybody would agree in praising the sort that consists in acquiring new aptitudes, but many moderns look with suspicion upon the sort that consists in pretence. Daydreams, in adult life, are recognized as more or less pathological, and as a substitute for efforts in the sphere of reality. Some of the discredit which has fallen upon daydreams has spilled over on to children's pretences, quite mistakenly, as I think. Montessori teachers do not like children to turn their apparatus into trains or steamers or what not: this is called "disordered imagination". They are quite right, because what the children are doing is not really play, even if to themselves it may seem to be nothing more. The apparatus amuses the child, but its purpose is instruction; the amusement is merely a means to instruction. In real play, amusement is the governing purpose. When the objection to "disordered imagination" is carried over into genuine play, it seems to me to go too far. The same thing applies to the objection to telling children about fairies and giants and witches and magic carpets and so on. I cannot sympathize with the ascetics of truth, any more than with ascetics of other kinds. It is commonly said that children do not distinguish between pretence and reality, but I see very little reason to believe this. We do not believe that Hamlet ever existed, but we should be annoyed by a man who kept reminding us of this while we were enjoying the play. So children are annoyed by a tactless reminder of reality, but are not in the least taken in by their own make-believe.

Truth is important, and imagination is important; but imagination develops earlier in the history of the individual, as in that of the race. So long as the child's physical needs are attended to, he finds games far more interesting than reality. In games he is a king: indeed he rules his territory with a power surpassing that of any mere earthly monarch. In reality he has to go to bed at a certain time, and to obey a host of tiresome precepts. He is exasperated when unimaginative adults interfere thoughtlessly with his *mise-en-scène*. When he has built a wall that not even the biggest giants can scale, and you carelessly step over it, he is as angry as Romulus was with Remus. Seeing that his inferiority to other people is normal, not pathological, its compensation in fantasy is also normal and not pathological. His games do not take up time which might be more profitably spent in other ways: if all his hours were given over to serious pursuits, he would soon become a nervous wreck. An adult who indulges in dreams may be told to exert himself in order to realize them; but a child cannot yet realize dreams which it is right that he should have. He does not regard his fancies as a permanent substitute for reality; on the contrary, he ardently hopes to translate them into fact when the time comes.

It is a dangerous error to confound truth with matter-of-fact. Our life is governed not only by facts, but by hopes; the kind of truthfulness which sees nothing but facts is a prison for the human spirit. Dreams are only to be condemned when they are a lazy substitute for an effort to change reality; when they are an incentive, they are fulfilling a vital purpose in the incarnation of human ideals. To kill fancy in childhood is to make a slave to what exists, a creature tethered to earth and therefore unable to create heaven.

This is all very well, you may say, but what has it to do with giants eating children, or Bluebeard cutting off his wives' heads? Are these things to exist in your heaven? Must not imagination be purified and ennobled before it can serve any good purpose? How can you, a pacifist, allow your innocent boy to revel in the thought of destroying human life? How can you justify a pleasure derived from instincts of

savagery which the human race must outgrow?
All this I imagine the reader has been feeling.
The matter is important, and I will try to state
why I hold to a different point of view.

Education consists in the cultivation of instincts, not in their suppression. Human
instincts are very vague, and can be satisfied in
a great variety of ways. Most of them require,
for their gratification, some kind of skill.
Cricket and baseball satisfy the same instinct,
but a boy will play whichever he has learnt.
Thus the secret of instruction, in so far as it
bears upon character, is to give a man such kinds
of skill as shall lead to his employing his instincts usefully. The instinct of power, which
in the child is crudely satisfied by identification
with Bluebeard, can find in later life a refined
satisfaction by scientific discovery, or artistic
creation, or the creation and education of
splendid children, or any one of a thousand
useful activities. If the only thing a man knows
is how to fight, his will to power will make him
delight in battle. But if he has other kinds of
skill, he will find his satisfaction in other ways.
If, however, his will to power has been nipped
in the bud when he was a child, he will be list-
less and lazy, doing little good and little harm;
he will be *"a Dio spiacente ed a' nemici sui."*
This kind of milksop goodness is not what the
world needs, or what we should try to produce

in our children. While they are small and cannot do much harm, it is biologically natural that
they should, in imagination, live through the
life of remote savage ancestors. Do not be
afraid that they will remain at that level, if you
put in their way the knowledge and skill required for more refined satisfactions. When I
was a child, I loved to turn head over heels. I
never do so now, though I should not think it
wicked to do so. Similarly the child who enjoys
being Bluebeard will outgrow this taste, and
learn to seek power in other ways. And if his
imagination has been kept alive in childhood by
the stimuli appropriate to that stage, it is much
more likely to remain alive in later years, when
it can exercise itself in the ways suitable to a
man. It is useless to obtrude moral ideas at an
age at which they can evoke no response, and
at which they are not yet required for the control of behaviour. The only effect is boredom,
and imperviousness to those same ideas at the
later age when they might have become potent.
That is one reason, among others, why the study
of child-psychology is of such vital importance
to education.

The games of later years differ from those
of early childhood by the fact that they become
increasingly competitive. At first, a child's play
is solitary; it is difficult for an infant to join in
the games of older brothers and sisters. But

collective play, as soon as it becomes possible, is so much more delightful that pleasure in playing alone quickly ceases. English upper-class education has always attributed an enormous moral importance to school games. To my mind, there is some exaggeration in the conventional British view, although I admit that games have certain important merits. They are good for health, provided they are not too expert; if exceptional skill is too much prized the best players overdo it, while the others tend to lapse into spectators. They teach boys and girls to endure hurts without making a fuss, and to incur great fatigue cheerfully. But the other advantages which are claimed for them seem to me largely illusory. They are said to teach co-operation, but in fact they only teach it in its competitive form. This is the form required in war, not in industry or in the right kind of social relations. Science has made it technically possible to substitute co-operation for competition, both in economics and in international politics; at the same time it has made competition (in the form of war) much more dangerous than it used to be. For these reasons, it is more important than in former times to cultivate the idea of co-operative enterprises in which the "enemy" is physical nature, rather than competitive enterprises in which there are human victors and vanquished. I do not want to lay too much stress upon this consideration, because competitiveness is natural to man and must find some outlet, which can hardly be more innocent than games and athletic contests. This is a valid reason for not preventing games, but it is not a valid reason for exalting them into a leading position in the school curriculum. Let boys play because they like to do so, not because the authorities think games an antidote to what the Japanese call "dangerous thoughts".

I have said a great deal in an earlier chapter about the importance of overcoming fear and producing courage; but courage must not be confounded with brutality. Brutality is pleasure in forcing one's will upon other people; courage is indifference to personal misfortunes. I would teach boys and girls, if opportunity offered, to sail small ships in stormy seas, to dive from heights, to drive a motor-car or even an aeroplane. I would teach them, as Sanderson of Oundle did, to build machines and incur risks in scientific experiment. As far as possible, I would represent inanimate nature as the antagonist in the game; the will to power can find satisfaction in this contest just as well as in competing with other human beings. The skill acquired in this way is more useful than skill in cricket or football, and the character developed is more in accordance with social morality. And apart from moral qualities, the cult of athletics involves an under-estimation of intelligence. Great Britain is losing her industrial position, and will perhaps lose her empire, through stupidity, and through the fact that the authorities do not value or promote intelligence. All this is connected with the fanatical belief in the paramount importance of games. Of course it goes deeper: the belief that a young man's athletic record is a test of his worth is a symptom of our general failure to grasp the need of knowledge and thought in mastering the complex modern world. But on this topic I will say no more now, as it will be considered again at a later stage.

There is another aspect of school games, which is usually considered good but which I think on the whole bad; I mean, their efficacy in promoting *esprit de corps*. *Esprit de corps* is liked by authorities, because it enables them to utilize bad motives for what are considered to be good actions. If efforts are to be made they are easily stimulated by promoting the desire to surpass some other group. The difficulty is that no motive is provided for efforts which are not competitive. It is amazing how deeply the competitive motive has eaten into all our activities. If you wish to persuade a borough to improve the public provision for the care of children, you have to point out that some neighbouring borough has a lower infant mortality. If you wish to persuade a manufacturer to adopt a new process which is clearly an improvement, you have to emphasize the danger of competition. If you wish to persuade the War Office that a modicum of military knowledge is desirable in the higher commands—but no, not even fear of defeat will prevail in this case, so strong is the "gentlemanly" tradition.[2] Nothing is done to promote constructiveness for its own sake, or to make people take an interest in doing their job efficiently even if no one is to be injured thereby. Our economic system has more to do with this than school games. But school games, as they now exist, embody the spirit of competition. If the spirit of co-operation is to take its place, a change in school games will be necessary. But to develop this subject would take us too far from our theme. I am not considering the building of the good State, but the building of the good individual, in so far as this is possible in the existing State. Improvement in the individual and improvement in the community must go hand in hand, but it is the individual that specially concerns the writer on education.

[2] See *e.g.* "The Secret Corps", by Captain Ferdinand Tuohy, Chap. VI, (Murray, 1920).

CHAPTER VI

CONSTRUCTIVENESS

THE subject of this chapter is one which has already been considered incidentally in connection with play, but it is now to be considered on its own account.

The instinctive desires of children, as we have seen, are vague; education and opportunity can turn them into many different channels. Neither the old belief in original sin, nor Rousseau's belief in natural virtue, is in accordance with the facts. The raw material of instinct is ethically neutral, and can be shaped either to good or evil by the influence of the environment. There is ground for a sober optimism in the fact that, apart from pathological cases, most people's instincts are, at first, capable of being developed into good forms; and the pathological cases would be very few, given proper mental and physical hygiene in the early years. A proper education would make it possible to live in accordance with instinct, but it would be a trained and cultivated instinct, not the crude unformed impulse which

is all that nature provides. The great culti-
vator of instinct is skill: skill which provides
certain kinds of satisfaction, but not others.
Give a man the right kinds of skill, and he will
be virtuous; give him the wrong kinds, or none
at all, and he will be wicked.

These general considerations apply with
special force to the will to power. We all like
to effect *something*, but so far as the love of
power is concerned we do not care what we
effect. Broadly speaking, the more difficult
the achievement the more it pleases us. Men
like fly-fishing, because it is difficult; they will
not shoot a bird sitting, because it is easy. I
take these illustrations, because in them a man
has no ulterior motive beyond the pleasure of
the activity. But the same principle applies
everywhere. I liked arithmetic until I learnt
Euclid, Euclid until I learnt analytical geometry, and so on. A child, at first, delights in
walking, then in running, then in jumping
and climbing. What we can do easily no longer
gives us a sense of power; it is the newly-
acquired skill, or the skill about which we are
doubtful, that gives us the thrill of success.
That is why the will to power is so immeasur-
ably adaptable according to the type of skill
which is taught.

Construction and destruction alike satisfy
the will to power, but construction is more diffi-

cult as a rule, and therefore gives more satisfaction to the person who can achieve it. I shall not attempt to give a pedantically exact definition of construction and destruction; I suppose, roughly speaking, we construct when we increase the potential energy of the system in which we are interested, and we destroy when we diminish its potential energy. Or, in more psychological terms, we construct when we produce a predesigned structure, and we destroy when we liberate natural forces to alter an existing structure, without being interested in the resulting new structure. Whatever may be thought of these definitions, we all know in practice whether an activity is to be regarded as constructive or destructive, except in a few cases where a man professes to be destroying with a view to rebuilding and we are not sure whether he is sincere.

Destruction being easier, a child's games usually begin with it, and only pass on to construction at a later stage. A child on the sand with a pail likes grown-up people to make sand-puddings, and then knock them down with his spade. But as soon as he can make sand-puddings himself, he delights in doing so, and will not permit them to be knocked down. When a child first has bricks, he likes to destroy towers built by his elders. But when he has learnt to build for himself, he becomes inordinately proud of his performances, and cannot bear to see his architectural efforts reduced to a heap of ruins. The impulse which makes the child enjoy the game is exactly the same at both stages, but new skill has changed the activity resulting from the impulse.

The first beginnings of many virtues arise out of experiencing the joys of construction. When a child begs you to leave his constructions undestroyed, you can easily make him understand that he must not destroy other people's. In this way you can create respect for the produce of labour, the only socially innocuous source of private property. You also give the child an incentive to patience, persistence, and observation; without these qualities, he will not succeed in building his tower to the height upon which he had set his heart. In play with children, you should only construct yourself sufficiently to stimulate ambition and to show how the thing is done; after that, construction should be left to their own efforts.

If a child has access to a garden, it is easy to cultivate a more elaborate form of constructiveness. The first impulse of a child in a garden is to pick every attractive flower. It is easy to check this by prohibition, but mere prohibition is inadequate as an education. One wants to produce in the child the same respect for the garden that restrains the grown-ups from picking wantonly. The respect of the grown-up is due to realization of the labour and effort required to produce the pleasing result. By the time a child is three years old, he can be given a corner of the garden and encouraged to plant seeds in it. When they come up and blossom, his own flowers seem precious and wonderful; then he can appreciate that his mother's flowers also must be treated with care.

The elimination of thoughtless cruelty is to be effected most easily by developing an interest in construction and growth. Almost every child, as soon as he is old enough, wants to kill flies and other insects; this leads on to the killing of larger animals, and ultimately of men. In the ordinary English upper-class family, the killing of birds is considered highly creditable, and the killing of men in war is regarded as the noblest of professions. This attitude is in accordance with untrained instinct: it is that of men who possess no form of constructive skill, and are therefore unable to find any innocent embodiment of their will to power. They can make pheasants die and tenants suffer; when occasion arises, they can shoot a rhinoceros or a German. But in more useful arts they are entirely deficient, as their parents and teachers thought it sufficient to make them into English gentlemen. I do not believe that at birth they are any stupider than other babies; their deficiencies in later life are entirely attributable to bad education. If, from an early age, they had been led to feel the value of life by watching its development with affectionate proprietorship; if they had acquired forms of constructive skill; if they had been made to realize with apprehension how quickly and easily a slow product of anxious solicitude can be destroyed —if all this had formed part of their early moral training, they would not be so ready to destroy what others have similarly created or tended. The great educator in this respect in later life is parenthood, provided the instinct is adequately aroused. But in the rich this seldom happens, because they leave the care of their children to paid professionals; therefore we cannot wait till they become parents before beginning to eradicate their destructive tendencies.

Every author who has had uneducated housemaids knows that it is difficult (the public may wish it were impossible) to restrain their passion for lighting the fire with his manuscripts. A fellow-author, even if he were a jealous enemy, would not think of doing such a thing, because experience has taught him the value of manuscripts. Similarly the boy who has a garden will not trample on other people's flower-beds, and the boy who has pets can be taught to respect animal life. Respect for human life is likely to exist in any one who has taken trouble over his or her own children. It is the trouble we take over our children that elicits the stronger forms of parental affection; in those who avoid this trouble the parental instinct becomes more or less atrophied, and remains only as a sense of responsibility. But parents are far more likely to take trouble over their children if their own constructive impulses have been fully developed; thus for this reason also it is very desirable to pay attention to this aspect of education.

When I speak of constructiveness, I am not thinking only of material construction. Such occupations as acting and choral singing involve co-operative non-material construction; they are pleasant to many children and young people, and should be encouraged (though not enforced). Even in purely intellectual matters it is possible to have a constructive or a destructive bias. A classical education is almost entirely critical: a boy learns to avoid mistakes, and to despise those who commit them. This tends to produce a kind of cold correctness, in which originality is replaced by respect for authority. Correct Latin is fixed once for all: it is that of Vergil and Cicero. Correct science is continually changing, and an able youth may look forward to helping in this process. Consequently the attitude produced by a scientific education is likely to be more constructive than that produced by the study of dead languages. Wherever avoidance of error is the chief thing aimed at, education tends to produce an intellectually bloodless type. The prospect of doing something venturesome with one's knowledge ought to be held before all the abler young men and young women. Too often, higher education is regarded as conferring something analogous to good manners, a merely negative code by which solecisms are avoided. In such an education, constructiveness has been forgotten. The usual type produced is, as might be expected, niggling, unenterprising, and lacking in generosity. All this is avoided when positive achievement is made the goal of education.

In the later years of education, there should be a stimulation of social constructiveness. I mean, that those whose intelligence is adequate should be encouraged in using their imaginations to think out more productive ways of utilizing existing social forces or creating new ones. Men read Plato's "Republic", but they do not attach it to current politics at any point. When I stated that the Russian State in 1920 had ideals which were almost exactly those of the "Republic", it was hard to say whether the Platonists or the Bolsheviks were the more shocked. People read a literary classic without any attempt to see what it means in terms of the lives of Brown, Jones and Robinson. This is particularly easy with a Utopia, because we are not told of any road which leads to it from our present social system. The valuable faculty, in these matters, is that of judging rightly as to the next step. British nineteenth-century Liberals had this merit, though the ultimate results to which their measures were bound to lead would have horrified them. A great deal depends upon the kind of image that dominates a man's thinking, often quite unconsciously. A social system may be conceived in many ways; the commonest are a mould, a machine, and a tree. The first belongs to the static conceptions of society, such as those of Sparta and traditional China: human nature is to be poured into a prepared mould, and to set in a preconceived shape. Something of this idea exists in any rigid moral or social convention. The man whose outlook is dominated by this image will have a political outlook of a certain kind—stiff and unyielding, stern and persecuting. The man who conceives of society as a machine is more modern. The industrialist and the communist alike belong to this class. To them, human nature is uninteresting, and the ends of life are simple—usually the maximizing of production. The purpose of social organization is to secure these simple ends. The difficulty is that actual human beings will not desire them; they persist in wanting all kinds of chaotic things which seem worthless to the tidy mind of the organizer. This drives the organizer back to the mould, in order to produce human beings who desire what he thinks good. And this, in turn, leads to revolution.

The man who imagines a social system as a tree will have a different political outlook. A bad machine can be scrapped, and another put in its place. But if a tree is cut down, it is a long time before a new tree achieves the same strength and size. A machine or a mould is what its maker chooses; a tree has its specific nature, and can only be made into a better or worse example of the species. Constructiveness applied to living things is quite different from constructiveness applied to machines; it has humbler functions, and requires a sort of sympathy. For that reason, in teaching constructiveness to the young, they should have opportunities of exercising it upon plants and animals, not only upon bricks and machines. Physics has been dominant in thought since the time of Newton, and in practice since the industrial revolution; this has brought with it a rather mechanical conception of society. Biological evolution introduced a new set of ideas, but they were somewhat overshadowed by natural selection, which it should be our aim to eliminate from human affairs by eugenics, birth-control, and education. The conception of society as a tree is better than the mould or the machine, but it is still defective. It is to psychology that we must look to supply the deficiency. Psychological constructiveness is a new and special kind, very little understood as yet. It is essential to a right theory of education, politics, and all purely human affairs. And it should dominate the imaginations of citizens, if they are not to be misled by false analogies. Some people dread constructiveness in human affairs, because they fear that it must be mechanical; they therefore believe in anarchism and the "return to nature". I am trying in this book to show, in concrete instances, how psychological construction differs from the construction of a machine. The imaginative side of this idea ought to be made familiar in higher education; if it were, I believe that our politics would cease to be angular and sharp and destructive, becoming instead supple and truly scientific, with the development of splendid men and women as its goal.

CHAPTER VII

SELFISHNESS AND PROPERTY

I COME now to a problem analogous to that
of Fear, in that we are concerned with an impulse which is strong, partly instinctive, and
largely undesirable. In all such cases, we have
to be careful not to thwart a child's nature. It
is useless to shut our eyes to his nature, or to
wish that it were different; we must accept the
raw material which is provided, and not attempt to treat it in ways only applicable to some
different material.

Selfishness is not an ultimate ethical conception; the more it is analysed, the vaguer it becomes. But as a phenomenon in the nursery it
is perfectly definite, and presents problems with
which it is very necessary to cope. Left to himself, an older child will seize a younger child's
toys, demand more than his share of grown-up
attention, and generally pursue his desires re-
gardless of the younger child's disappointments.
A human ego, like a gas, will always expand
unless restrained by external pressure. The
object of education, in this respect, is to let the

external pressure take the form of habits, ideas and sympathies in the child's own mind, not of knocks and blows and punishments. The idea which is needed is that of justice, not self-sacrifice. Every person has a right to a certain amount of room in the world, and should not be made to feel wicked in standing up for what is due to him. When self-sacrifice is taught, the idea seems to be that it will not be fully practised, and that the practical result will be about right. But in fact people either fail to learn the lesson, or feel sinful when they demand mere justice, or carry self-sacrifice to ridiculous extremes. In the last case, they feel an obscure resentment against the people to whom they make renunciations, and probably allow selfishness to return by the back door of a demand for gratitude. In any case, self-sacrifice cannot be true doctrine, because it cannot be universal; and it is most undesirable to teach falsehood as a means to virtue, because when the falsehood is perceived the virtue evaporates. Justice, on the contrary, can be universal. Therefore justice is the conception that we ought to try to instil into the child's thoughts and habits.

It is difficult, if not impossible, to teach justice to a solitary child. The rights and desires of grown-up people are so different from those of children that they make no imaginative appeal; there is hardly ever direct competition for exactly the same pleasure. Moreover, as the grown-up people are in a position to exact obedience to their own demands, they have to be judges in their own case, and do not produce upon the child the effect of an impartial tribunal. They can, of course, give definite precepts inculcating this or that form of convenient behaviour: not to interrupt when their mother is counting the wash, not to shout when their father is busy, not to obtrude their concerns when there are visitors. But these are inexplicable requirements, to which, it is true, the child submits willingly enough if otherwise kindly treated, but which make no appeal to his own sense of what is reasonable. It is right that the child should be made to obey such rules, because he must not be allowed to be a tyrant, and because he must understand that other people attach importance to their own pursuits, however odd those pursuits may be. But not much more than external good behaviour is to be got by such methods; the real education in justice can only come where there are other children. This is one of many reasons why no child should long be solitary. Parents who have the misfortune to have an only child should do all that they can to secure companionship for it, even at the cost of a good deal of separation from home, if no other way is possible. A solitary child must be either suppressed or selfish—perhaps both by turns. A well-behaved only child is pathetic, and an ill-behaved one is a nuisance. In these days of small families, this is a more serious trouble than it used to be. It is one of the grounds for advocating nursery-schools, as to which I shall have more to say in a later chapter. But for the moment I shall assume a family of two at least, not very widely separated in age, so that their tastes are largely the same.

Where there is competition for a pleasure which can only be enjoyed by one at a time, such as a ride in a wheelbarrow, it will be found that the children readily understand justice. Their impulse, of course, is to demand the pleasure for themselves to the exclusion of the others, but it is surprising how quickly this impulse is overcome when the grown-ups institute the system of a turn for each. I do not believe that a sense of justice is innate, but I have been astonished to see how quickly it can be created. Of course, it must be real justice; there must not be any secret bias. If you are fonder of some of the children than of others, you must be on your guard to prevent your affections from having any influence on your distribution of pleasures. It is of course a generally recognized principle that toys must be equal.

It is quite useless to attempt to suppress the

demand for justice by any kind of moral training. Do not give more than justice, but do not
expect the child to accept less. There is a
chapter in "The Fairchild Family" on "The
Secret Sins of the Heart" which illustrates the
methods to be avoided. Lucy has maintained
that she has been good, so her mother tells her
that even when her behaviour is all right her
thoughts are wrong, and quotes: "The heart
is deceitful above all things and desperately
wicked" (Jeremiah, xvii, 9). So Mrs. Fairchild gives Lucy a little book in which to record
the "desperately wicked" things that are in her
heart when outwardly she is good. At break-
fast, her parents give a ribbon to her sister and a
cherry to her brother, but nothing to her. She
records in her book that at this point she had a
very wicked thought, that her parents loved her
brother and sister better than they loved her.
She had been taught, and she believed, that she
ought to cope with this thought by moral discipline; but by this method it could only be driven
underground, to produce strange distorted effects in later years. The proper course would
have been for her to express her feeling, and
for her parents to dispel it either by giving her
a present, too, or by explaining, in a way she
could understand, that she must wait for another time, as no further present was available
at the moment. Truth and frankness dispel

difficulties, but the attempt at repressive moral discipline only aggravates them.

Closely connected with justice is the sense of property. This is a difficult matter, which must be dealt with by adaptable tact, not by any rigid set of rules. There are, in fact, conflicting considerations, which make it difficult to take a clear line. On the one hand, the love of property produces many terrible evils in later years; the fear of losing valued material possessions is one of the main sources of political and economic cruelty. It is desirable that men and women should, as far as possible, find their happiness in ways which are not subject to private ownership, *i.e.*, in creative rather than defensive activities. For this reason, it is unwise to cultivate the sense of property in children if it can be helped. But before proceeding to act upon this view, there are some very strong arguments on the other side, which it would be dangerous to neglect. In the first place, the sense of property is very strong in children; it develops as soon as they can grasp objects which they see (the hand-eye co-ordination). What they grasp, they feel is theirs, and they are indignant if it is taken away. We still speak of a property as a "holding", and "maintenance" means "holding in the hand". These words show the primitive connection between property and grasp; so does the word "grasping".

A child which has no toys of its own will pick up sticks or broken bricks or any odds and ends it may find, and will treasure them as its very own. The desire for property is so deep-seated that it cannot be thwarted without danger. Moreover property cultivates carefulness and curbs the impulse of destruction. Especially useful is property in anything that the child has made himself; if this is not permitted, his constructive impulses are checked.

Where the arguments are so conflicting, we cannot adopt any clear-cut policy, but must be guided to a great extent by circumstances and the child's nature. Nevertheless, something can be said as to the means of reconciling these opposites in practice.

Among toys, some should be private and some common. To take an extreme case, a rocking-horse would of course always be common. This suggests a principle: where a toy can be equally enjoyed by all, but only by one at a time, it should be common if it is too large or expensive to be duplicated. On the other hand, toys more adapted to one child than to another (because of difference of age, for example) may properly belong to the one to whom they give the most pleasure. If a toy wants careful handling which an older child has learnt to give, it is fair that a younger child should not be allowed to get hold of it and spoil it. The younger child should be compensated by private property in the toys specially appropriate to its age. After two years old, a broken toy should not be immediately replaced if it has been broken by the child's carelessness; it is just as well that the loss should be felt for a while. Do not let a child always refuse the use of its own toys to other children. Whenever it has more than it can actually use, it should not be allowed to protest if another child plays with those that it is not using. But here I should except toys which the other child is likely to break, and toys out of which their owner has constructed some edifice which is a source of pride. Until the edifice is forgotten, it should, if possible, be allowed to stand, as a reward of industry. Subject to these provisos, do not let the child develop a dog-in-the-manger attitude; it must never be allowed to prevent another child's enjoyment wantonly. It is not very difficult to teach a modicum of decent behaviour in these respects, and it is quite worth the necessary firmness. Do not allow a child to snatch things from another child, even when it would be within its legal rights in doing so. If an older child is unkind to a younger one, show a similar unkindness to the older one, and explain immediately why you do so. By such methods it is not difficult to establish that degree of kindness in children to each other which is necessary to prevent constant storms and tears. On occasion, a certain amount of sternness may be necessary, amounting to a mild form of punishment. But on no account must a habit of tyrannizing over the weak be allowed to develop.

While permitting a certain number of cherished possessions, it is well to encourage the habit of using toys, such as bricks, to which the child only has the exclusive right while he is using them. The Montessori apparatus is common to all the children, but so long as a child is using one piece of apparatus no other child must interfere. This develops a sense of limited tenant-right, dependent upon work; such a sense does not run counter to anything that is desirable in later years. For very young children, this method is hardly applicable, because they are not yet sufficiently constructive. But as they acquire skill it becomes more and more possible to interest them in the process of building. So long as they know they can have the material for construction whenever they like, they will not much mind others having it too, and the reluctance to sharing which they may feel at first is soon dispelled by custom. Nevertheless, when a child is old enough, he should, I think, be allowed to own books, because that will increase his love of books and therefore stimulate reading. The books that are his own property should, as far as possible, be good books, such as Lewis Carroll and Tanglewood Tales, not mere trash. If the children want trash, it should be common property.

The broad principles involved are: First, do not produce in the child a sense of thwarting from not having enough property; this is the way to produce a miser. Secondly, allow the child private property when it stimulates a desirable activity, and, in particular, where it teaches careful handling. But subject to these limitations turn the child's attention, as far as you can, to pleasures not involving private ownership. And even where there is private ownership, do not allow the child to be mean or miserly when other children wish to be allowed to play with his things. As to this, however, the object is to induce the child to lend of his own free will; so long as authority is required, the end aimed at has not been achieved. In a happy child, it should not be difficult to stimulate a generous disposition; but if the child is starved of pleasures, he will of course cling tenaciously to those that are attainable. It is not through suffering that children learn virtue, but through happiness and health.

CHAPTER VIII

TRUTHFULNESS

To produce the habit of truthfulness should be one of the major aims of moral education. I do not mean truthfulness in speech only, but also in thought; indeed, of the two, the latter seems to me the more important. I prefer a person who lies with full consciousness of what he is doing to a person who first sub-consciously deceives himself and then imagines that he is being virtuous and truthful. Indeed, no man who thinks truthfully can believe that it is *always* wrong to speak untruthfully. Those who hold that a lie is always wrong have to supplement this view by a great deal of casuistry and considerable practice in misleading ambiguities, by means of which they deceive without admitting to themselves that they are lying. Nevertheless, I hold that the occasions when lying is justifiable are few—much fewer than would be inferred from the practice of high-minded men. And almost all the occasions which justify lying are occasions where power is being used tyrannically, or where people are engaged in some harmful activity such as war; therefore in a good social system they would be even rarer than they are now.

Untruthfulness, as a practice, is almost always a product of fear. The child brought up without fear will be truthful, not in virtue of a moral effort, but because it will never occur to him to be otherwise. The child who has been treated wisely and kindly has a frank look in the eyes, and a fearless demeanour even with strangers; whereas the child that has been subject to nagging or severity is in perpetual terror of incurring reproof, and terrified of having transgressed some rule whenever he has behaved in a natural manner. It does not at first occur to a young child that it is possible to lie. The possibility of lying is a discovery, due to observation of grown-ups quickened by terror. The child discovers that grown-ups lie to him, and that it is dangerous to tell them the truth; under these circumstances he takes to lying. Avoid these incentives, and he will not think of lying.

But in judging whether children are truthful, a certain caution is necessary. Children's memories are very faulty, and they often do not know the answer to a question when grown-up people think they do. Their sense of time is very vague; a child under four will hardly distinguish between yesterday and a week ago, or between yesterday and six hours ago. When they do not know the answer to a question, they tend to say yes or no according to the suggestion in your tone of voice. Again, they are often talking in the dramatic character of some make-believe. When they tell you solemnly that there is a lion in the back garden, this is obvious; but in many cases it is quite easy to mistake play for earnest. For all these reasons, a young child's statements are often objectively untrue, but without the slightest intention to deceive. Indeed, children tend, at first, to regard grown-ups as omniscient, and therefore incapable of being deceived. My boy (three and three quarters) will ask me to tell him (for the pleasure of the story) what occurred to him on some interesting occasion when I was not present; I find it almost impossible to persuade him that I don't know what happened. Grown-up people get to know so many things in ways the child does not understand, that he cannot set limits to their powers. Last Easter, my boy was given a number of chocolate Easter eggs. We told him that if he ate too much chocolate. he would be sick, but, having told him, we left him alone. He ate too much, and was sick. He came to me as soon as the crisis was over, with a beaming face, saying, in a voice almost of triumph, "I was sick, Daddy—Daddy told me I should be sick." His pleasure in the verification of a scientific law was astonishing. Since then, it has been possible to trust him with chocolate, in spite of the fact that he seldom has it; moreover he implicitly believes everything we tell him about what food is good for him. There has been no need of moral exhortation or punishment or fear in bringing about this result. There has been need, at earlier stages, of patience and firmness. He is nearing the age where it is usual for boys to steal sweet things and lie about it. I dare say he will steal sometimes, but I shall be surprised if he lies. When a child does lie, parents should take themselves to task rather than him; they should deal with it by removing its causes, and by explaining gently and reasonably why it is better not to lie. They should not deal with it by punishment, which only increases fear and therefore the motive for lying.

Rigid truthfulness in adults towards children is, of course, absolutely indispensable if children are not to learn lying. Parents who teach that lying is a sin, and who nevertheless are known to lie by their children, naturally lose all moral authority. The idea of speaking the truth to children is entirely novel; hardly anybody did it before the present generation. I greatly doubt whether Eve told Cain and Abel the truth about apples; I am convinced that she told them she had never eaten anything that wasn't good for her. It used to be the thing for parents to represent themselves as Olympians, immune from human passions and always actuated by pure reason. When they reproached the children, they did it more in sorrow than in anger; however they might scold, they were not "cross", but talking to the children for their good. Parents did not realize that children are astonishingly clear-sighted: they do not understand all the solemn political reasons for humbug, but despise it straightforwardly and simply. Jealousies and envies of which you are unconscious will be evident to your child, who will discount all your fine moral talk about the wickedness of the objects of these passions. Never pretend to be faultless and inhuman; the child will not believe you, and would not like you any the better if he did. I remember vividly how, at a very early age, I saw through the Victorian humbug and hypocrisy with which I was surrounded, and vowed that, if I ever had children, I would not repeat the mistakes that were being made with me. To the best of my ability, I am keeping this vow.

Another form of lying, which is extremely bad for the young, is to threaten punishments you do not mean to inflict. Dr. Ballard, in his most interesting book on "The Changing School",[1] has stated this principle rather em-

[1] Hodder and Stoughton, 1925.

phatically: "Don't threaten. If you do, let
nothing stop you from carrying out your threat.
If you say to a boy, 'Do that again and I'll murder you', and he does it again, then you must
murder him. If you don't he will lose all respect for you" (p. 112,). The punishments
threatened by nurses and ignorant parents in
dealing with infants are somewhat less extreme,
but the same rule applies. Do not insist, except
for good reason; but when you have once begun
insisting, continue, however you may regret
having embarked upon the battle. If you
threaten a punishment, let it be one that you are
prepared to inflict; never trust to luck that your
bluff will not be called. It is odd how difficult
it is to get this principle understood by uneducated people. It is particularly objectionable
when they threaten something terrifying, such
as being locked up by the policeman or carried
off by the bogey-man. This produces first a
state of dangerous nervous terror and then a
complete scepticism as to all statements and
threats by grown-up people. If you never insist without carrying the matter through, the
child soon learns that on such occasions resistance is useless, and he obeys a mere word without giving further trouble. But it is essential
to the success of this method that you should
not insist unless there is some really strong
reason for doing so.

Another undesirable form of humbug is to treat inanimate objects as if they were alive. Nurses sometimes teach children, when they have hurt themselves by bumping into a chair or table, to smack the offending object and say, "naughty chair" or "naughty table". This removes a most useful source of natural discipline. Left to himself, the child soon realizes that inanimate objects can only be manipulated by skill, not by anger or cajolery. This is a stimulus to the acquisition of skill, and a help in realizing the limits of personal power.

Lies about sex are sanctioned by time-honoured usage. I believe them to be wholly and utterly bad, but I shall say no more on this subject now, as I propose to devote a chapter to sex education.

Children who are not suppressed ask innumerable questions, some intelligent, others quite the reverse. These questions are often wearisome, and sometimes inconvenient. But they must be answered truthfully, to the best of your ability. If the child asks you a question connected with religion, say exactly what you think, even if you contradict some other grown-up person who thinks differently. If he asks you about death, answer him. If he asks you questions designed to show that you are wicked or foolish, answer him. If he asks you about war, or capital punishment, answer him. Do not put him off with "you can't understand that yet", except in difficult scientific matters, such as how electric light is made. And even then, make it clear that the answer is a pleasure in store for him, as soon as he has learnt rather more than he now knows. Tell him rather more than he can understand, not rather less; the part he fails to understand will stimulate his curiosity and his intellectual ambition.

Invariable truthfulness to a child reaps its reward in increased trust. The child has a natural tendency to believe what you say, except when it runs counter to a strong desire, as in the case of the Easter eggs which I mentioned just now. A little experience of the truth of your remarks even in these cases enables you to win belief easily and without emphasis. But if you have been in the habit of threatening consequences which did not happen, you will have to become more and more insistent and terrifying, and in the end you will only produce a state of nervous uncertainty. One day my boy wanted to paddle in a stream, but I told him not to, because I thought there were bits of broken crockery which would cut his feet. His desire was keen, so he was sceptical about the crockery; but after I had found a piece and shown him the sharp edge, he became entirely acquiescent. If I had invented the crockery for my own convenience, I should have lost his confidence. If I had not found any, I should have let him paddle. In consequence of repeated experiences of this sort, he has almost entirely ceased to be sceptical of my reasons.

We live in a world of humbug, and the child brought up without humbug is bound to despise much that is commonly thought to deserve respect. This is regrettable, because contempt is a bad emotion. I should not call his attention to such matters, though I should satisfy his curiosity whenever it turned towards them. Truthfulness is something of a handicap in a hypocritical society, but the handicap is more than outweighed by the advantages of fearlessness, without which no one can be truthful. We wish our children to be upright, candid, frank, self-respecting; for my part, I would rather see them fail with these qualities than succeed by the arts of the slave. A certain native pride and integrity is essential to a splendid human being, and where it exists lying becomes impossible, except when it is prompted by some generous motive. I would have my children truthful in their thoughts and words, even if it should entail worldly misfortune, for something of more importance than riches and honours is at stake.

CHAPTER IX

PUNISHMENT

In former days, and until very recently, the punishment of children, both boys and girls, was taken as a matter of course, and was universally regarded as indispensable in education. We have seen in an earlier chapter what Dr. Arnold thought about flogging, and his views were, at the time, exceptionally humane. Rousseau is associated with the theory of leaving things to nature, yet in "Emile" he occasionally advocates quite severe punishments. The conventional view, a hundred years ago, is set forth in one of the "Cautionary Tales", in which a little girl makes a fuss because they are putting on her white sash when she wants her pink one.

> Papa, who in the parlour heard
> Her make the noise and rout,
> That instant went to Caroline,
> To whip her, there's no doubt.

When Mr. Fairchild found his children quarrelling, he caned them, making the cane keep time to the verse "Let dogs delight to bark and bite". He then took them to see a corpse hanging in chains on a gibbet. The little boy was frightened, and begged to be taken home, as the chains rattled in the wind. But Mr. Fairchild compelled him to look for a long time, saying that this spectacle showed what happened to those who had hatred in their hearts. The child was destined to become a clergyman, and presumably had to be taught to depict the terrors of the damned with the vividness of one who has experienced them.

Nowadays, few people would advocate such methods, even in Tennessee. But there is considerable divergence of opinion as to what should take their place. Some people still advocate a fair amount of punishment, while others consider that it is possible to dispense with punishment altogether. There is room for many shades between these two extremes.

For my part, I believe that punishment has a certain very minor place in education; but I doubt whether it need ever be severe. I include speaking sharply or reprovingly among punishments. The most severe punishment that ought ever to be necessary is the natural spontaneous expression of indignation. On a few occasions when my boy has been rough with his younger sister, his mother has expressed anger by an impulsive exclamation. The effect has been very great. The boy burst into sobs, and would not be consoled until his mother had made much of him. The impression was very profound, as one could see from his subsequent good conduct towards his sister. On a few occasions we have resorted to mild forms of punishment when he has persisted in demanding things we had refused him, or in interfering with his sister's play. In such cases, when reason and exhortation have failed, we take him to a room by himself, leave the door open, and tell him he can come back as soon as he is good. In a very few minutes, after crying vigorously, he comes back, and is invariably good: he perfectly understands that in coming back he has undertaken to be good. So far, we have never found any need of severer penalties. If one can judge from the books of old-fashioned disciplinarians, the children educated by the old methods were far naughtier than the modern child. I should certainly be horrified if my boy were half as badly behaved as the children in "The Fairchild Family"; but I should think the fault lay more with his parents than with himself. I believe that reasonable parents create reasonable children. The children must feel their parents' affection—not duty and responsibility, for which no child is grateful, but warm love, which feels delight in the child's presence and ways. And except when it is quite impossible, a prohibition must be explained carefully and

truthfully. Small misfortunes, such as bruises
and slight cuts, should sometimes be allowed to
happen rather than interfere with rash games;
a little experience of this kind makes children
more willing to believe that a prohibition may
be wise. Where these conditions are present
from the first, I believe children will seldom
do anything deserving of serious punishment.

When a child persistently interferes with
other children or spoils their pleasures, the obvious penalty is banishment. It is imperatively
necessary to take steps of some kind, because it
would be most unfair to let the other children
suffer. But there is no use in making the re-
fractory child feel guilty; it is much more to
the purpose to make him feel that he is missing pleasures which the others are enjoying.
Madame Montessori describes her practice as
follows:

As to punishments, we have many times come in
contact with children who disturbed the others without paying attention to our corrections. Such children were at once examined by the physician. When
the case proved to be that of a normal child, we
placed one of the little tables in a corner of the
room, and in this way isolated the child; having him
sit in a comfortable little armchair, so placed that
he might see his companions at work, and giving
him those games and toys to which he was most
attracted. This isolation almost always succeeded in
calming the child; from his position he could see the

entire assembly of his companions, and the way in which they carried on their work was an *object lesson* much more efficacious than any words of the teacher could possibly have been. Little by little, he would come to see the advantages of being one of the company working so busily before his eyes, and he would really wish to go back and do as the others did. We have in this way led back again to discipline all the children who at first seemed to rebel against it. The isolated child was always made the object of special care, almost as if he were ill. I myself, when I entered the room, went first of all directly to him, as if he were a very little child. Then I turned my attention to the others, interesting myself in their work, asking questions about it as if they had been little men. I do not know what happened in the soul of these children whom we found it necessary to discipline, but certainly the conversion was always very complete and lasting. They showed great pride in learning how to work and how to conduct themselves, and always showed a very tender affection for the teacher and for me.[1]

The success of this method depended upon several factors not present in old-fashioned schools. There was first the elimination of those whose bad conduct was due to some medical defect. Then there was tact and skill in applying the method. But the really vital point was the good conduct of the majority of the class: the child felt itself opposed to the public opinion which it naturally respected.

[1] "The Montessori Method" (Heinemann, 1912), p. 103.

This is, of course, an entirely different situation from that of the schoolmaster who has a class bent on "ragging". I do not propose to discuss the methods which he should employ, because they would never be needed if education were properly conducted from the start. Children like to learn things, provided they are the right things properly taught. The same mistake is made in imparting knowledge as is made, at an earlier stage, in regard to food and sleep: something which is really an advantage to the child is made to appear like a favour to the adult. Infants easily come to think that the only reason for eating and sleeping is that grown-ups desire it; this turns them into dyspeptic sufferers from insomnia.[2] Unless a child is ill, let it leave its food and go hungry. My boy had been coaxed into eating by his nurse, and had grown more and more *difficile*. One day when we had him for his mid-day meal, he refused to eat his pudding, so we sent it out. After a while, he demanded it back, but it turned out that the cook had eaten it. He was flabbergasted, and never made such pretences with us again. Exactly the same method should apply to instruction. Those who do not want it should be allowed to go without, though I should see to it that they were bored if they were absent during lesson time. If they see

[2] See Dr. H. C. Cameron, "The Nervous Child", Chaps. IV and V.

others learning, they will presently clamour to be taught: the teacher can then appear as conferring a benefit, which is the truth of the situation. I should have in every school a large bare room to which pupils could go if they did not want to learn, but if they went there, I should not allow them to come back to lessons that day. And they should be sent there as a punishment if they behaved badly in lesson-time. It seems a simple principle that a punishment should be something you wish the culprit to dislike, not something you wish him to like. Yet "lines" are a common punishment where the professed aim is to produce a love of classical literature.

Mild punishments have their utility for dealing with mild offences, especially such as are concerned with manners. Praise and blame are an important form of rewards and punishments for young children, and also for older boys and girls if conferred by a person who inspires respect. I do not believe it possible to conduct education without praise and blame, but in regard to both a certain degree of caution is necessary. In the first place, neither should be comparative. A child should not be told that he has done better than so-and-so, or that such-and-such is never naughty: the first produces contempt, the second hatred. In the second place, blame should be given much more sparingly than praise; it should be a definite punishment, administered for some unexpected lapse from good behaviour, and it should never be continued after it has produced its effect. In the third place, praise should not be given for anything that should be a matter of course. I should give it for a new development of courage or skill, and for an act of unselfishness as regards possessions, if achieved after a moral effort. All through education, any unusually good piece of work should be praised. To be praised for a difficult achievement is one of the most delightful experiences in youth, and the desire for this pleasure is quite proper as an added incentive, though it should not be the main motive. The main motive should always be an interest in the matter itself, whatever the matter may happen to be.

Grave faults of character, such as cruelty, can seldom be dealt with by means of punishment. Or rather, punishment should be a very small part of the treatment. Cruelty to animals is more or less natural to boys, and requires, for its prevention, an education *ad hoc*. It is a very bad plan to wait until you find your boy torturing an animal, and then proceed to torture the boy. This only makes him wish he had not been caught. You should watch for the first beginnings of what may afterwards develop into cruelty. Teach the boy respect for life; do not let him see you killing animals, even wasps or snakes. If you cannot prevent it, explain very carefully why it is done in this particular case. If he does something slightly unkind to a younger child, do the same to him at once. He will protest, and you can explain that if he does not want it done to him he must not do it to others. In this way the fact that others have feelings like his own is brought vividly to his attention.

It is obviously essential to this method that it should be begun early, and applied to minor forms of unkindness. It is only very small injuries to others that you can retort in kind upon the child. And when you can adopt this plan, do not let it seem that you are doing it as a punishment, but rather as an instruction: "See, that is what you did to your little sister." When the child protests, you say: "Well, if it was unpleasant, you mustn't do it to her." So long as the whole incident is simple and immediate, the child will understand, and will learn that other people's feelings must be considered. In that case, serious cruelty will never develop.

All moral instruction must be immediate and concrete: it must arise out of a situation which has grown up naturally, and must not go beyond what ought to be done in this particular instance. The child himself will apply the moral in other similar cases. It is much easier to grasp a con-

crete instance, and apply analogous considerations to an analogous instance, than to apprehend a general rule and proceed deductively.
Do not say, in a general way, "Be brave, be
kind", but urge him to some particular piece of
daring, and then say, "Bravo, you were a brave
boy"; get him to let his sister play with his
mechanical engine, and when he sees her beaming with delight, say, "That's right, you were
a kind boy." The same principle applies in
dealing with cruelty: Look out for its faint
beginnings, and prevent them from developing.

If, in spite of all your efforts, grave cruelty
develops at a later age, the matter must be taken
very seriously, and dealt with like an illness.
The boy should be punished in the sense that
unpleasant things should happen to him, just as
they do when he has measles, but not in the sense
that he should be made to feel wicked. He
should be isolated for a while from other
children and from animals, and it should be
explained to him that it is not safe to let him
associate with them. He should be made to
realize, as far as possible, how he would suffer
if he were cruelly treated. He should be made
to feel that a great misfortune had befallen
him in the shape of an impulse to cruelty, and
that his elders were endeavouring to shield him
from a similar misfortune in the future. I
believe that such methods would be completely

successful in all except a few pathological cases.

Physical punishment I believe to be never right. In mild forms, it does little harm, though no good; in severe forms, I am convinced that it generates cruelty and brutality. It is true that it oftens produces no resentment against the person who inflicts it; where it is customary, boys adapt themselves to it and expect it as part of the course of nature. But it accustoms them to the idea that it may be right and proper to inflict physical pain for the purpose of maintaining authority—a peculiarly dangerous lesson to teach to those who are likely to acquire positions of power. And it destroys that relation of open confidence which ought to exist between parents and children, as well as between teachers and pupils. The modern parent wants his children to be as unconstrained in his presence as in his absence; he wants them to feel pleasure when they see him coming; he does not want a fictitious Sabbath calm while he is watching, succeeded by pandemonium as soon as he turns his back. To win the genuine affection of children is a joy as great as any that life has to offer. Our grandfathers did not know of this joy, and therefore did not know that they were missing it. They taught children that it was their "duty" to love their parents, and proceeded to make this duty almost impossible of performance. Caroline, in the verse quoted at the beginning of this chapter, can hardly have been pleased when her father went to her, "to whip her, there's no doubt". So long as people persisted in the notion that love could be commanded as a duty, they did nothing to win it as a genuine emotion. Consequently human relations remained stark and harsh and cruel. Punishment was part of this whole conception. It is strange that men who would not have dreamed of raising their hand against a woman were quite willing to inflict physical torture upon a defenceless child. Mercifully, a better conception of the relations of parents and children has gradually won its way during the last hundred years, and with it the whole theory of punishment has been transformed. I hope that the enlightened ideas which begin to prevail in education will gradually spread to other human relations as well, for they are needed there just as much as in our dealings with our children.

CHAPTER X

So far, we have been considering what parents and teachers can do themselves towards creating the right kind of character in a child. But there is a great deal that cannot possibly be done without the help of other children. This becomes increasingly true as the child gets older; indeed contemporaries are never more important than at the university. In the first year of life, other children are not important at all in the earlier months, and only a slight advantage in the last three months. At that stage, it is slightly older children that are useful. The first child in a family is usually slower in learning to walk and talk than subsequent children, because grown-ups are so perfect in these accomplishments that they are difficult to imitate. A child of three years old is a better model for a child one year old, both because the things it does are more what the younger child would wish to do, and because its powers do not seem so superhuman. Children feel that other children are more akin to them than adults are, and therefore their ambition is more stimulated by what other children do. Only the family provides the opportunity for this early education by older children. Most children who have a choice wish to play with children rather older than themselves, because then they feel "grand"; but these older children wish to play with still older children, and so on. The consequence is that, in a school, or in the streets of a slum, or anywhere else where a large choice is possible, children play almost entirely with their contemporaries, because the older ones will not play with the younger ones. In this way it comes about that what is to be learnt from older children must be learnt mainly in the home. This has the drawback that in every family there must be one oldest child, who fails to get the benefits of the method. And as families grow smaller, the percentage of oldest children grows larger, so that the drawback is an increasing one. Small families are in some ways a disadvantage to children, unless supplemented by nursery schools. But nursery schools will form the subject of a later chapter.

Older children, younger children, and contemporaries all have their uses, but the uses of older and younger children, for the reasons just given, are mainly confined to the family. The great use of older children is to provide attainable ambitions. A child will make tremendous efforts to be thought worthy of joining in an older child's game. The older child behaves in an offhand natural way, without the consideration and make-believe which is bound to form part of a grown-up person's games with children. The same lack of consideration in a grown-up would be painful, both because the grown-up has power and authority, and because he plays to please the child, not to please himself. A child will be cheerfully submissive to an older brother or sister, in a way which would be impossible towards an adult except as a result of excessive discipline. The lesson of co-operation in a subordinate role is best learnt from other children; when grown-ups try to teach it, they are faced with the opposite dangers of unkindness and pretence—unkindness if they demand real co-operation, pretence if they are content with the appearance of it. I do not mean that either real or pretence co-operation is to be always avoided, but that it has not the spontaneity which is possible between an older and a younger child, and therefore cannot be combined for hours on end with pleasure to both parties.

All through youth, slightly older people continue to have a special use in teaching—not formal teaching, but the sort which occurs outside working hours. A slightly older boy or girl remains always a very effective stimulus to am-

bition, and, if kind, can explain difficulties better than an adult, from the recent recollection
of overcoming them. Even at the university,
I learnt much from people a few years senior
to me, which I could not have learnt from grave
and reverend signors. I believe this experience
is general wherever the social life of the university is not too rigidly stratified by "years". It
is, of course, impossible where, as too often
happens, the older students consider it *infra dig*
to have anything to do with the younger ones.

Younger children also have their uses, especially in the years from three to six; these
uses are chiefly in connection with moral education. So long as a child is with adults, it has
no occasion for the exercise of a number of important virtues, namely, those required by the
strong in dealing with the weak. A child has
to be taught not to take things by force from a
younger brother or sister, not to show excessive
anger when the junior inadvertently knocks
over his tower of bricks, not to hoard toys he is
not using which the other desires. He has to
be taught that the junior can be easily hurt by
rough handling, and to feel compunction when
he has wantonly caused tears. In protecting
a younger child, one can speak to the senior
with a sharpness and suddenness which would
not otherwise be justified, but which have their
uses through the strong impression produced by

their unexpectedness. All these are useful lessons, which it is hardly possible to give naturally
in any other way. It is a folly and a waste of
time to give abstract moral instruction to a
child; everything must be concrete, and actually
demanded by the existing situation. Much that,
from an adult point of view, is moral education,
feels to the child just like instruction in handling a saw. The child feels that he is being
shown how the thing is done. That is one reason why example is so important. A child who
has watched a carpenter at work tries to copy
his movements; a child who has seen his parents
behaving always with kindness and consideration tries to copy them in this respect. In each
case, prestige is attached to what he wants to
imitate. If you gave your child a solemn lesson
in the use of a saw, but yourself always tried
to use it as a chopper, you would never make a
carpenter of him. And if you urge him to be
kind to his little sister, but are not kind to her
yourself, all your instruction will be wasted.
For that reason, when you have to do something
that makes a little child cry, such as cleaning
its nose, you should be careful to explain to the
older child why it is necessary to do it. Otherwise he is quite likely to rise up in defence of
the younger child, and fight you to make you
stop being cruel. If you allow him to remain
under the impression that you are cruel, you

will have lost the power to curb his own impulses towards tyranny.

Although both older and younger children are important, contemporaries are far more so, at any rate from the age of four onwards. Behaviour to equals is what most needs to be learnt. Most of the inequalities in the existing world are artificial, and it would be a good thing if our behaviour ignored them. Well-to-do people imagine themselves superior to their cooks, and behave to them in a different way from that in which they behave in society. But they feel inferior to a Duke, and treat him in a way which shows a lack of self-respect. In both cases they are wrong: the cook and the Duke should both be felt and treated as equals. In youth, age makes a hierarchy which is not artificial; but for that very reason the social habits which will be desirable in later life are best learnt by associating with contemporaries. Games of all kinds are better among equals, and so is school competition. Among schoolfellows, a boy has that degree of importance which is accorded to him by their judgment; he may be admired or despised, but the issue depends upon his own character and prowess. Affectionate parents create a too indulgent milieu; parents without affection create one where spontaneity is repressed. It is only contemporaries who can give scope for spontaneity in free competition and in equal co-operation.   Self-respect without tyranny, consideration without slavishness, can be learnt best in dealing with equals.   For these reasons, no amount of parental solicitude can give a boy or girl the same advantages at home as are to be enjoyed in a good school.

Apart from these considerations, there is another, perhaps even more important.   The mind and body of a child demand a great deal of play, and after the first years play can hardly be satisfactory except with other boys and girls. Without play, a child becomes strained and nervous; it loses the joy of life and develops anxieties.   It is, of course, possible to bring up a child as John Stuart Mill was brought up, to begin Greek at the age of three, and never know any ordinary childish fun.   From the mere standpoint of acquiring knowledge, the results may be good, but taken all round I cannot admire them.   Mill relates in his Autobiography that during adolescence he nearly committed suicide from the thought that all combinations of musical notes would one day be used up, and then new musical composition would become impossible.   It is obvious that an obsession of this sort is a symptom of nervous exhaustion.   In later life, whenever he came upon an argument tending to show that his father's philosophy might have been mistaken, he shied away from it like a frightened horse, thereby greatly di-

minishing the value of his reasoning powers. It
seems probable that a more normal youth would
have given him more intellectual resilience, and
enabled him to be more original in his thinking.
However that may be, it would certainly have
given him more capacity for enjoying life. I
was myself the product of a solitary education
up to the age of sixteen—somewhat less fierce
than Mill's, but still too destitute of the ordinary joys of youth. I experienced in adolescence just the same tendency to suicide as Mill
describes—in my case, because I thought the
laws of dynamics regulated the movements of
my body, making the will a mere delusion.
When I began to associate with contemporaries,
I found myself an angular prig. How far I
have remained so, it is not for me to say.

In spite of all the above arguments, I am
prepared to admit that there are a certain number of boys and girls who ought not to go to
school, and that some of them are very important individuals. If a boy has abnormal
mental powers in some direction, combined with
poor physique and great nervousness, he may be
quite incapable of fitting into a crowd of normal
boys, and may be so persecuted as to be driven
mad. Exceptional capacities are not infrequently associated with mental instability, and
in such cases it is desirable to adopt methods
which would be bad for the normal boy. Care

should be taken to find out if abnormal sensitiveness has some definite cause, and patient efforts should be made to cure it. But these efforts should never involve terrible suffering, such as an abnormal boy may easily have to endure from brutal companions. I think such sensitiveness generally has its source in mistakes during infancy, which have upset the child's digestion or its nerves. Given wisdom in handling infants, I think almost all of them would grow into boys and girls sufficiently normal to enjoy the company of other boys and girls. Nevertheless, some exceptions will occur, and they may easily occur among those who have some form of genius. In these rare cases, school is undesirable, and a more sheltered youth is to be preferred.

CHAPTER XI

AFFECTION AND SYMPATHY

MANY readers may think that I have hitherto
unaccountably neglected affection, which is, in
some sense, the essence of a good character. I
hold that love and knowledge are the two main
requisites for right action, yet, in dealing with
moral education, I have hitherto said nothing
about love. My reason has been that the right
sort of love should be the natural fruit resulting
from the proper treatment of the growing child,
rather than something consciously aimed at
throughout the various stages. We have to be
clear as to the kind of affection to be desired,
and as to the disposition appropriate to different
ages. From ten or twelve years old until puberty, a boy is apt to be very destitute of affection, and there is nothing to be gained by trying
to force his nature. Throughout youth, there is
less occasion for sympathy than in adult life,
both because there is less power of giving effective expression to it, and because a young person
has to think of his or her own training for life,
largely to the exclusion of other people's inter-

ests.   For these reasons, we should be more concerned to produce sympathetic and affectionate
adults than to force a precocious development
of these qualities in early years.   Our problem,
like all problems in the education of character,
is a scientific one, belonging to what may be
called psychological dynamics.   Love cannot
exist as a duty: to tell a child that it *ought* to
love its parents and its brothers and sisters is
utterly useless, if not worse.   Parents who wish
to be loved must behave so as to elicit love, and
must try to give to their children those physical
and mental characteristics which produce ex-
pansive affections.

Not only must children not be commanded
to love their parents, but nothing must be done
which has this result as its object.   Parental
affection, at its best, differs from sex love in
this respect.   It is of the essence of sex love
to seek a response, as is natural, since, without
a response, it cannot fulfil its biological function.   But it is not of the essence of parental
love to seek a response.   The natural unsophis-
ticated parental instinct feels towards the child
as towards an externalized part of the parent's
body.   If your great toe is out of order, you
attend to it from self-interest, and you do not
expect it to feel grateful.   The savage woman,
I imagine, has a very similar feeling towards
her child.   She desires its welfare in just the

same way as she desires her own, especially while it is still very young. She has no more sense of self-denial in looking after the child than in looking after herself; and for that very reason she does not look for gratitude. The child's need of her is sufficient response so long as it is helpless. Later, when it begins to grow up, her affection diminishes and her demands may increase. In animals, parental affection ceases when the child is adult, and no demands are made upon it; but in human beings, even if they are very primitive, this is not the case. A son who is a lusty warrior is expected to feed and protect his parents when they are old and decrepit; the story of Æneas and Anchises embodies this feeling at a higher level of culture. With the growth of foresight, there is an increasing tendency to exploit children's affections for the sake of their help when old age comes. Hence the principle of filial piety, which has existed throughout the world and is embodied in the Fifth Commandment. With the development of private property and ordered government, filial piety becomes less important; after some centuries, people become aware of this fact, and the sentiment goes out of fashion. In the modern world, a man of fifty may be financially dependent upon a parent of eighty, so that the important thing is still the affection of the parent for the child rather than of the child for the parent. This, of course, applies chiefly to the propertied classes; among wage-earners, the older relationship persists. But even there it is being gradually displaced as a result of old-age pensions and similar measures. Affection of children for parents, therefore, is ceasing to deserve a place among cardinal virtues, while affection of parents for children remains of enormous importance.

There is another set of dangers, which has been brought to the fore by the psycho-analysts, though I think their interpretation of the facts may be questioned. The dangers I am thinking of are those connected with undue devotion to one or other parent. An adult, and even an adolescent, ought not to be so overshadowed by either father or mother as to be unable to think or feel independently. This may easily happen if the personality of the parent is stronger than that of the child. I do not believe that there is, except in rare morbid cases, an "Œdipus Complex", in the sense of a special attraction of sons to mothers and daughters to fathers. The excessive influence of the parent, where it exists, will belong to the parent who has had most to do with the child—generally the mother—without regard to difference of sex. Of course, it may happen that a daughter who dislikes her mother and sees little of her father will idealize the latter; but in that case the influence is exerted by dreams, not by the actual father. Idealization consists of hanging hopes to a peg: the peg is merely convenient, and has nothing to do with the nature of the hopes. Undue parental influence is quite a different thing from this, since it is connected with the actual person, not with an imaginary portrait.

An adult with whom a child is in constant contact may easily become so dominant in the child's life as to make the child, even in later life, a mental slave. The slavery may be intellectual, or emotional, or both. A good example of the former is John Stuart Mill, who could never bring himself, in the last resort, to admit that his father might have been mistaken. To some degree, intellectual slavery to early environment is normal; very few adults are capable of opinions other than those taught by parents or teachers, except where there is some general drift that carries them along. The children of Mohammedans are Mohammedans, the children of Buddhists are Buddhists, and so on. It may be maintained that intellectual slavery is natural and normal; I am inclined to admit that it can only be avoided by an education *ad hoc*. This form of excessive parental and scholastic influence ought to be avoided carefully, since, in a rapidly changing world, it is exceedingly dangerous to retain the opinions of a by-gone generation. But for the present

I shall consider only slavery of the emotions and the will, since that is more directly bound up with our present topic.

The evils considered by psycho-analysts under the heading "Œdipus Complex" (which I regard as misleading) arise from an undue desire on the part of parents for an emotional response from their children. As I said a moment ago, I believe that the parental instinct in its purity does not desire an emotional response; it is satisfied by the dependence of the young, and the fact that they look to parents for protection and food. When the dependence ceases, parental affection also ceases. This is the state of affairs among animals, and for their purposes it is entirely satisfactory. But such simplicity of instinct is scarcely possible for human beings. I have already considered the effect of military and economic considerations, as shown in the preaching of filial piety. I am now concerned with two purely psychological sources of confusion in the working of the parental instinct.

The first of these is of a sort which occurs wherever intelligence observes the pleasures to be derived from instinct. Broadly speaking, instinct prompts pleasant acts which have useful consequences, but the consequences may not be pleasant. Eating is pleasant, but digestion is not—especially when it is indigestion. Sex is pleasant, but parturition is not. The dependence of an infant is pleasant, but the independence of a vigorous grown-up son is not. The primitive maternal type of woman derives most pleasure from the infant at the breast, and gradually less pleasure as the child grows less helpless. There is therefore a tendency, for the sake of pleasure, to prolong the period of helplessness, and to put off the time when the child can dispense with parental guidance. This is recognized in conventional phrases, such as being "tied to his mother's apron-strings". It was thought impossible to deal with this evil in boys except by sending them away to school. In girls it was not recognized as an evil, because (if they were well-to-do) it was thought desirable to make them helpless and dependent, and it was hoped that after marriage they would cling to their husbands as they had formerly clung to their mothers. This seldom happened, and its failure gave rise to the "mother-in-law" joke. One of the purposes of a joke is to prevent thought—a purpose in which this particular joke was highly successful. No one seemed to realize that a girl brought up to be dependent would naturally be dependent upon her mother, and therefore could not enter into that wholehearted partnership with a man which is the essence of a happy marriage.

The second psychological complication comes

nearer to the orthodox Freudian point of view.
It arises where elements appropriate to sex-love
enter into parental affection.   I do not mean
anything necessarily dependent upon difference
of sex; I mean merely the desire for a certain
kind of emotional response.   Part of the psychology of sex—that part, in fact, which has
made monogamy a possible institution—is the
desire to come first for some one, to feel that
oneself is more important than any other human
being to the happiness of at least one person in
the world.   When this desire has produced
marriage, it will only produce happiness if a
number of other conditions are realized.   For
one reason or another, a very large proportion
of married women in civilized countries fail to
have a satisfying sex-life.   When this happens
to a woman, she is apt to seek from her children
an illegitimate and spurious gratification of
desires which only men can gratify adequately
and natural.   I do not mean anything obvious:
I mean merely a certain emotional tension, a
certain passionateness of feeling, a pleasure in
kissing and fondling to excess.   These things
used to be thought quite right and proper in an
affectionate mother.   Indeed, the difference
between what is right and what is harmful is
very subtle.   It is absurd to maintain, as some
Freudians do, that parents ought not to kiss and
fondle their children at all.   Children have a

right to warm affection from their parents; it gives them a happy, care-free outlook upon the world, and is essential to healthy psychological development. But it should be something that they take for granted, like the air they breathe, not something to which they are expected to respond. It is this question of response that is the essence of the matter. There will be a certain spontaneous response, which is all to the good; but it will be quite different from the active pursuit of friendship from childish companions. Psychologically, parents should be a background, and the child should not be made to act with a view to giving his parents pleasure. Their pleasure should consist in his growth and progress; anything that he gives them in the way of response should be accepted gratefully as a pure extra, like fine weather in spring, but should not be expected as part of the order of nature.

It is very difficult for a woman to be a perfect mother, or a perfect teacher of young children, unless she is sexually satisfied. Whatever psycho-analysts may say, the parental instinct is essentially different from the sex instinct, and is damaged by the intrusion of emotions appropriate to sex. The habit of employing celibate female teachers is quite wrong psychologically. The right woman to deal with children is a woman whose instinct is not seeking from them satisfactions for herself which they ought not to be expected to provide. A woman who is happily married will belong to this type without effort; but any other woman will need an almost impossible subtlety of self-control. Of course, the same thing applies to men in the same circumstances, but the circumstances are far less frequent with men, both because their parental instincts are usually not very strong, and because they are seldom sexually starved.

It is as well to be clear in our own thoughts as regards the attitude we are to expect from children to parents. If parents have the right kind of love for their children, the children's response will be just what the parents desire. The children will be pleased when their parents come, and sorry when they go, unless they are absorbed in some agreeable pursuit; they will look to their parents for help in any trouble, physical or mental, that may arise; they will dare to be adventurous, because they rely upon their parents' protection in the background— but this feeling will be hardly conscious except in moments of peril. They will expect their parents to answer their questions, resolve their perplexities, and help them in difficult tasks. Most of what their parents do for them will not enter into their consciousness. They will like their parents, not for providing their board and lodging, but for playing with them, showing them how to do new things, and telling them stories about the world. They will gradually realize that their parents love them, but this ought to be accepted as a natural fact. The affection that they feel for their parents will be quite a different kind from that which they feel for other children. The parent must act with reference to the child, but the child must act with reference to himself and the outer world. That is the essential difference. The child has no important function to perform in relation to his parents. His function is to grow in wisdom and stature, and so long as he does so a healthy parental instinct is satisfied.

I should be very sorry to convey the impression that I want to diminish the amount of affection in family life, or the spontaneity of its manifestations. That is not at all what I mean. What I do mean is that there are different kinds of affection. The affection of husband and wife is one thing, that of parents for children is another, and that of children for parents is yet another. The harm comes when these different kinds of natural affection are confused. I do not think the Freudians have arrived at the truth, because they do not recognize these instinctive differences. And this makes them, in a sense, ascetic as regards parents and children, because they view any love between them as a sort of inadequate sex-love. I do not believe in the need of any fundamental self-denial, provided there are no special unfortunate circumstances. A man and woman who love each other and their children ought to be able to act spontaneously as the heart dictates. They will need much thought and knowledge, but these they will acquire out of parental affection. They must not demand from their children what they get from each other, but if they are happy in each other they will feel no impulse to do so. If the children are properly cared for, they will feel for their parents a natural affection which will be no barrier to independence. What is needed is not ascetic self-denial, but freedom and expansiveness of instinct, adequately informed by intelligence and knowledge.

When my boy was two years and four months old, I went to America, and was absent three months. He was perfectly happy in my absence, but was wild with joy when I returned. I found him waiting impatiently by the garden gate; he seized my hand, and began showing me everything that specially interested him. I wanted to hear, and he wanted to tell; I had no wish to tell, and he had none to hear. The two impulses were different, but harmonious. When it comes to stories, he wishes to hear and I wish to tell, so that again there is harmony. Only once has this situation been reversed. When

he was three years and six months old, I had a
birthday, and his mother told him that everything was to be done to please me.   Stories are
his supreme delight; to our surprise, when the
time for them came, he announced that he was
going to tell me stories, as it was my birthday.
He told about a dozen, then jumped down,
saying "no more stories to-day".   That was
three months ago, but he has never told stories
again.

I come now to the wider question of affection
and sympathy in general.   As between parents
and children, there are complications owing to
the possibility of abuse of power by parents;
it was necessary to deal with these complications
before attacking the general question.

There is no possible method of *compelling* a
child to feel sympathy or affection; the only
possible method is to observe the conditions
under which these feelings arise spontaneously,
and then endeavour to produce the conditions.
Sympathy, undoubtedly, is partly instinctive.
Children are worried when their brothers or
sisters cry, and often cry too.   They will take
their part vehemently against the grown-ups
when disagreeable things are being done to
them.   When my boy had a wound on his elbow
which had to be dressed, his sister (aged eighteen months) could hear him crying in another
room, and was very much upset.   She kept on

repeating "Jonny crying, Jonny crying", until the painful business was finished. When my boy saw his mother extracting a thorn with a needle from her foot, he said anxiously, "It doesn't hurt, Mummy". She said it did, wishing to give him a lesson in not making a fuss. He insisted that it didn't hurt, whereupon she insisted that it did. He then burst into sobs, just as vehement as if it had been his own foot. Such occurrences must spring from instinctive physical sympathy. This is the basis upon which more elaborate forms of sympathy must be built. It is clear that nothing further is needed in the way of positive education except to bring home to the child the fact that people and animals can feel pain, and do feel it under certain circumstances. There is, however, a further negative condition: the child must not see people he respects committing unkind or cruel actions. If the father shoots or the mother speaks rudely to the maids, the child will catch these vices.

It is a difficult question how and when to make a child aware of the evil in the world. It is impossible to grow up ignorant of wars and massacres and poverty and preventable disease which is not prevented. At some stage, the child must know of these things, and must combine the knowledge with a firm conviction that it is a dreadful thing to inflict, or even permit, any suffering which can be avoided. We are here confronted by a problem similar to that which faces people who wish to preserve female chastity; these people formerly believed in ignorance till marriage, but now adopt more positive methods.

I have known some pacifists who wished history taught without reference to wars, and thought that children should be kept as long as possible ignorant of the cruelty in the world. But I cannot praise the "fugitive and cloistered virtue" that depends upon absence of knowledge. As soon as history is taught at all, it should be taught truthfully. If true history contradicts any moral we wish to teach, our moral must be wrong, and we had better abandon it. I quite admit that many people, including some of the most virtuous, find facts inconvenient, but that is due to a certain feebleness in their virtue. A truly robust morality can only be strengthened by the fullest knowledge of what really happens in the world. We must not run the risk that the young people whom we have educated in ignorance will turn to wickedness with delight as soon as they discover that there is such a thing. Unless we can give them an aversion from cruelty, they will not abstain from it; and they cannot have an aversion from it if they do not know that it exists.

Nevertheless, the right way of giving children a knowledge of evil is not easily found. Of course, those who live in the slums of big cities get to know early all about drunkenness, quarrels, wife-beating, and so on. Perhaps this does them no harm, if it is counteracted by other influences; but no careful parent would deliberately expose a very young child to such sights. I think the great objection is that they rouse fear so vividly as to colour the whole of the rest of life. A child, being defenceless, cannot help feeling terror when it first understands that cruelty to children is possible. I was about fourteen when I first read "Oliver Twist", but it filled me with emotions of horror which I could scarcely have borne at an earlier age. Dreadful things should not be known to young people until they are old enough to face them with a certain poise. This moment will come sooner with some children than with others: those who are imaginative or timid must be sheltered longer than those who are stolid or endowed with natural courage. A mental habit of fearlessness due to expectation of kindness should be firmly established before the child is made to face the existence of unkindness. To choose the moment and the manner requires tact and understanding; it is not a matter which can be decided by a rule.

There are, however, certain maxims which should be followed. To begin with, stories such as Bluebeard and Jack the Giant Killer do not involve any knowledge of cruelty whatever, and do not raise the problems we are considering. To the child, they are purely fantastic, and he never connects them with the real world in any way. No doubt the pleasure he derives from them is connected with savage instincts, but these are harmless as mere play-impulses in a powerless child, and they tend to die down as the child grows older. But when the child is first introduced to cruelty as a thing in the real world, care must be taken to choose incidents in which he will identify himself with the victim, not with the torturer. Something savage in him will exult in a story in which he identifies himself with the tyrant; a story of this kind tends to produce an imperialist. But the story of Abraham preparing to sacrifice Isaac, or of the she-bears killing the children whom Elisha cursed, naturally rouses the child's sympathy for another child. If such stories are told, they should be told as showing the depths of cruelty to which men could descend long ago. I once, as a child, heard a sermon of an hour's duration, entirely devoted to proving that Elisha was right in cursing the children. Fortunately, I was old enough to think the parson a fool; otherwise I should have been driven nearly mad with terror. The story of Abraham and Isaac was even more dreadful, because it was the child's father who was cruel to him. When such stories are told with the assumption that Abraham and Elisha were virtuous, they must either be ignored or utterly debase a child's moral standards. But when told as an introduction to human wickedness, they serve a purpose, because they are vivid, remote, and untrue. The story of Hubert putting out little Arthur's eyes, in "King John", may be used in the same way.

Then history may be taught, with all its wars. But in telling about wars, sympathy at first should be with the defeated. I should begin with battles in which it is natural to feel on the side of the beaten party—for instance, the battle of Hastings in teaching an English boy. I should emphasize always the wounds and suffering produced. I should gradually lead the child to feel no partisanship in reading about wars, and to regard both sides as silly men who had lost their tempers, and ought to have had nurses to put them to bed till they were good. I should assimilate wars to quarrels among the children in the nursery. In this way, I believe children could be made to see the truth about war, and to realize that it is silly.

If any actual instance of unkindness or cruelty comes under the child's notice, it should be fully discussed, with all the moral values which the adult himself attaches to the incident, and always with the suggestion that the people who acted cruelly were foolish, and did not know any better because they had not been well brought up. But I should not call the child's attention to such things in his real world, if they were not spontaneously observed by him, until after he had grown familiar with them in history and stories. Then I should gradually introduce him to a knowledge of evil in his surroundings. But I should always give him the feeling that the evil can be combated, and results from ignorance and lack of self-control and bad education. I should not encourage him to be indignant with malefactors, but rather to regard them as bunglers, who do not know in what happiness consists.

The cultivation of wide sympathies, given the instinctive germ, is mainly an intellectual matter: it depends upon the right direction of attention, and the realization of facts which militarists and authoritarians suppress. Take, for example, Tolstoy's description of Napoleon going round the battlefield of Austerlitz after the victory. Most histories leave the battle-field as soon as the battle is over; by the simple expedient of lingering on it for another twelve hours, a completely different picture of war is produced. This is done, not by suppressing facts, but by giving more facts. And what applies to battles applies equally to other forms of cruelty. In all cases, it should be quite unnecessary to point the moral; the right telling of the story should be sufficient. Do not moralize, but let the facts produce their own moral in the child's mind.

It remains to say a few words about affection, which differs from sympathy in being inevitably and essentially selective. I have spoken already of affection between parents and children; it is affection between equals that I now wish to consider.

Affection cannot be created; it can only be liberated. There is a kind of affection which is partly rooted in fear; affection for parents has this element, since parents afford protection. In childhood affections of this sort are natural, but in later life they are undesirable, and even in childhood affection for other children is not of this sort. My little girl is intensely devoted to her brother, although he is the only person in her world who ever treats her unkindly. Affection as to an equal, which is the best kind, is much more likely to exist where there is happiness and absence of fear. Fears, conscious or unconscious, are very apt to produce hatred, because other people are regarded as capable of inflicting injuries. With most people, as things are, envy is a barrier to wide-spread affection. I do not think envy can be prevented except by happiness; moral discipline is powerless to touch its subconscious forms. Happiness, in turn, is largely prevented by fear. Young people who have a chance of happiness are deterred by parents and "friends", nominally on moral grounds, but really from envy. If the young people have enough fearlessness, they will ignore the croakers; otherwise, they will allow themselves to be made miserable, and join the company of envious moralists. The education of character that we have been considering is designed to produce happiness and courage; I think, therefore, that it does what is possible to liberate the springs of affection. More than this cannot be done. If you tell children that they ought to be affectionate, you run the risk of producing cant and humbug. But if you make them happy and free, if you surround them with kindness, you will find that they become spontaneously friendly with everybody, and that almost everybody responds by being friendly with them. A trustful affectionate disposition justifies itself, because it gives irresistible charm, and creates the response which it expects. This is one of the most important results to be expected from the right education of character.

CHAPTER XII

THE subject of sex is so surrounded by super-stitions and taboos that I approach it with trepi-dation. I fear lest those readers who have hitherto accepted my principles may suspect them when they are applied in this sphere; they may have admitted readily enough that fear-lessness and freedom are good for a child, and yet desire, where sex is concerned, to impose slavery and terror. I cannot so limit principles which I believe to be sound, and I shall treat sex exactly as I have treated the other impulses which make up a human character.

There is one respect in which, quite inde-pendently of taboos, sex is peculiar, and that is the late ripening of the instinct. It is true, as the psycho-analysts have pointed out (though with considerable exaggeration), that the in-stinct is not absent in childhood. But its child-ish manifestations are different from those of adult life, and its strength is much less, and it is physically impossible for a boy to indulge it in the adult manner. Puberty remains an important emotional crisis, thrust into the middle of intellectual education, and causing disturbances which raise difficult problems for the educator. Many of these problems I shall not attempt to discuss; it is chiefly what should be done before puberty that I propose to consider. It is in this respect that educational reform is most needed, especially in very early childhood. Although I disagree with the Freudians in many particulars, I think they have done a very valuable service in pointing out the nervous disorders produced in later life by wrong handling of young children in matters connected with sex. Their work has already produced wide-spread beneficial results in this respect, but there is still a mass of prejudice to be overcome. The difficulty is, of course, greatly increased by the practice of leaving children, during their first years, largely in the hands of totally uneducated women, who cannot be expected to know, still less to believe, what has been said by learned men in the long words necessary to escape prosecution for obscenity.

Taking our problems in chronological order, the first that confronts mothers and nurses is that of masturbation. Competent authorities state that this practice is all but universal among boys and girls in their second and third years, but usually ceases of itself a little later on. Sometimes it is rendered more pronounced by some definite physical irritation which can be removed. (It is not my province to go into medical details.) But it usually exists even in the absence of such special reasons. It has been the custom to view it with horror, and to use dreadful threats with a view to stopping it. As a rule these threats do not succeed, although they are believed; the result is that the child lives in an agony of apprehension, which presently becomes dissociated from its original cause (now repressed into the unconscious), but remains to produce nightmares, nervousness, delusions and insane terrors. Left to itself, infantile masturbation has, apparently, no bad effect upon health[1], and no discoverable bad effect upon character; the bad effects which have been observed in both respects are, it seems, wholly attributable to attempts to stop it. Even if it were harmful, it would be unwise to issue a prohibition which is not going to be observed; and from the nature of the case, it is impossible to make sure that the child will not continue after you have forbidden him to do so. If you do nothing, the probability is that the practice will soon be discontinued. But if you do anything, you make it much less likely that it will cease, and you lay the foundation of terrible nervous disorders. Therefore, difficult as it

---

[1] In very rare instances, it does a little harm, but this is easily cured and is not more serious than the results of thumb-sucking.

may be, the child should be let alone in this respect. I do not mean that you should abstain from methods other than prohibition, in so far as they are available. Let him be sleepy when he goes to bed, so that he will not lie awake long. Let him have some favourite toy in bed, which may distract his attention. Such methods are quite unobjectionable. But if they fail, do not resort to prohibition, or even call his attention to the fact that he indulges in the practice. Then it will probably cease of itself.

Sexual curiosity normally begins during the third year, in the shape of an interest in the physical differences between men and women, and between adults and children. By nature, this curiosity has no special quality in early childhood, but is simply a part of general curiosity. The special quality which it is found to have in children who are being conventionally brought up is due to the grown-up practice of making mysteries. When there is no mystery, the curiosity dies down as soon as it is satisfied. A child should, from the first, be allowed to see his parents and brothers and sisters without their clothes whenever it so happens naturally. No fuss should be made either way; he should simply not know that people have feelings about nudity. (Of course, later on he will have to know.) It will be found that the child presently notices the differences between his father and mother, and connects them with the differences between brothers and sisters. But as soon as the subject has been explored to this extent, it becomes uninteresting, like a cupboard that is often open. Of course, any questions the child may ask during this period must be answered just as questions on other topics would be answered.

Answering questions is a major part of sex education. Two rules cover the ground. First, always give a truthful answer to a question; secondly, regard sex knowledge as exactly like any other knowledge. If the child asks you an intelligent question about the sun or the moon or the clouds, or about motor-cars or steam-engines, you are pleased, and you tell him as much as he can take in. This answering of questions is a very large part of early education. But if he asks you a question connected with sex, you will be tempted to say, "hush, hush". If you have learnt not to do that, you will still answer briefly and dryly, perhaps with a trifle of embarrassment in your manner. The child at once notices the *nuance*, and you have laid the foundations of prurience. You must answer with just the same fulness and naturalness as if the question had been about something else. Do not allow yourself to feel, even unconsciously, that there is something horrid and dirty about sex. If you do, your feeling will communicate itself to him. He will think, necessarily, that there is something nasty in the relations of his parents; later on, he will conclude that they think ill of the behaviour which led to his existence. Such feelings in youth make happy instinctive emotions almost impossible, not only in youth, but in adult life also.

If the child has a brother or sister born when he is old enough to ask questions about it, say after the age of three, tell him that the child grew in his mother's body, and tell him that he grew in the same way. Let him see his mother suckling the child, and be told that the same thing happened to him. All this, like everything else connected with sex, must be told without solemnity, in a purely scientific spirit. The child must not be talked to about "the mysterious and sacred functions of motherhood"; the whole thing must be utterly matter-of-fact.

If no addition to the family occurs when the child is old enough to ask questions about it, the subject is likely to arise out of being told "that happened before you were born". I find my boy still hardly able to grasp that there was a time when he did not exist; if I talk to him about the building of the Pyramids or some such topic, he always wants to know what he was doing then, and is merely puzzled when he is told that he did not exist. Sooner or later he will want to know what "being born" means, and then we shall tell him.

The share of the father in generation is less likely to come up naturally in answer to questions, unless the child lives on a farm. But it is very important that the child should know of this first from parents or teacher, not from children whom bad education has made nasty. I remember vividly being told all about it by another boy when I was twelve years old; the whole thing was treated in a ribald spirit, as a topic for obscene jokes. That was the normal experience of boys in my generation. It followed naturally that the vast majority continued through life to think sex comic and nasty, with the result that they could not respect a woman with whom they had intercourse, even though she were the mother of their children. Parents pursued a cowardly policy of trusting to luck, although fathers must have remembered how they gained their first knowledge. How it can have been supposed that such a system helped sanity or sound morals, I cannot imagine. Sex must be treated from the first as natural, delightful and decent. To do otherwise is to poison the relations of men and women, parents and children. Sex is at its best between a father and mother who love each other and their children. It is far better that children should first know of sex in the relations of their parents than that they should derive their first impressions from ribaldry. It is particularly bad that they should discover sex between their parents as a guilty secret which has been concealed from them.

If there were no likelihood of being taught badly about sex by other children, the matter could be left to the natural operation of the child's curiosity, and parents could confine themselves to answering questions—always provided that everything became known before puberty. This, of course, is absolutely essential. It is a cruel thing to let a boy or girl be overtaken by the physical and emotional changes of that time without preparation, and possibly with the feeling of being attacked by some dreadful disease. Moreover, the whole subject of sex, after puberty, is so electric that a boy or girl cannot listen in a scientific spirit, which is perfectly possible at an earlier age. Therefore, quite apart from the possibility of nasty talk, a boy or girl should know the nature of the sexual act before attaining puberty.

How long before this the information should be given depends upon circumstances. An inquisitive and intellectually active child must be told sooner than a sluggish child. There must at no time be unsatisfied curiosity. However young the child may be, he must be told if he asks. And his parents' manner must be such that he will ask if he wants to know. But if he does not ask spontaneously, he must in any case be told before the age of ten, for fear of being first told by others in a bad way. It may therefore be desirable to stimulate his curiosity by instruction about generation in plants and animals. There must not be a solemn occasion, a clearing of the throat, and an exordium: "Now, my boy, I am going to tell you something that it is time for you to know." The whole thing must be ordinary and every-day. That is why it comes best in answer to questions.

I suppose it is unnecessary at this date to argue that boys and girls must be treated alike. When I was young, it was still quite common for a "well-brought-up" girl to marry before knowing anything about the nature of marriage, and to have to learn it from her husband; but I have not often heard of such a thing in recent years. I think most people recognize nowadays that a virtue dependent upon ignorance is worthless, and that girls have the same right to knowledge as boys. If there are any who still fail to recognize this, they are not likely to read the present work, so that it is not worth while to argue with them.

I do not propose to discuss the teaching of sexual morality in the narrower sense. This is a matter as to which a variety of opinions exist.

Christians differ from Mohammedans, Catholics from Protestants who tolerate divorce, freethinkers from mediævalists. Parents will all wish their children taught the particular brand of sexual morality in which they believe themselves, and I should not wish the State to interfere with them. But without going into vexed questions, there is a good deal that might be common ground.

There is first of all hygiene. Young people must know about venereal disease before they run the risk of it. They should be taught about it truthfully, without the exaggerations which some people practise in the interests of morals. They should learn both how to avoid it, and how to cure it. It is a mistake to give only such instruction as is needed by the perfectly virtuous, and to regard the misfortunes which happen to others as a just punishment of sin. We might as well refuse to help a man who has been injured in a motoring accident, on the ground that careless driving is a sin. Moreover, in the one case as in the other, the punishment may fall upon the innocent; no one can maintain that children born with syphilis are wicked, any more than that a man is wicked if a careless motorist runs over him.

Young people should be led to realize that it is a very serious matter to have a child, and that it should not be undertaken unless the child has a reasonable prospect of health and happiness. The traditional view was that, within marriage, it is always justifiable to have children, even if they come so fast that the mother's health is ruined, even if the children are diseased or insane, even if there is no prospect of their having enough to eat. This view is now only maintained by heartless dogmatists, who think that everything disgraceful to humanity redounds to the glory of God. People who care for children, or do not enjoy inflicting misery upon the helpless, rebel against the ruthless dogmas which justify this cruelty. A care for the rights and importance of children, with all that is implied, should be an essential part of moral education.

Girls should be taught to expect that one day they are likely to be mothers, and they should acquire some rudiments of the knowledge that may be useful to them in that capacity. Of course both boys and girls ought to learn something of physiology and something of hygiene. It should be made clear that no one can be a good parent without parental affection, but that even with parental affection a great deal of knowledge is required as well. Instinct without knowledge is as inadequate in dealing with children as knowledge without instinct. The more the necessity of knowledge is understood, the more intelligent women will feel attracted to motherhood. At present, many highly educated women despise it, thinking that it does not give scope for the exercise of their intellectual faculties; this is a great misfortune, since they are capable of being the best mothers, if their thoughts were turned in that direction.

One other thing is essential in teaching about sex-love. Jealousy must not be regarded as a justifiable insistence upon rights, but as a misfortune to the one who feels it and a wrong towards its object. Where possessive elements intrude upon love, it loses its vivifying power and eats up personality; where they are absent, it fulfils personality and brings a greater intensity of life. In former days, parents ruined their relations with their children by preaching love as a duty; husbands and wives still too often ruin their relations to each other by the same mistake. Love cannot be a duty, because it is not subject to the will. It is a gift from heaven, the best that heaven has to bestow. Those who shut it up in a cage destroy the beauty and joy which it can only display while it is free and spontaneous. Here, again, fear is the enemy. He who fears to lose what makes the happiness of his life has already lost it. In this, as in other things, fearlessness is the essence of wisdom.

For this reason, in teaching my own children, I shall try to prevent them from learning a moral code which I regard as harmful. Some people who themselves hold liberal views are willing that their children shall first acquire conventional morals, and become emancipated only later, if at all. I cannot agree to this, because I hold that the traditional code not only forbids what is innocent, but also commends what is harmful. Those who have been taught conventionally will almost inevitably believe themselves justified in indulging jealousy when occasion arises; moreover they will probably be obsessed by sex either positively or negatively. I shall not teach that faithfulness to our partner through life is in any way desirable, or that a permanent marriage should be regarded as excluding temporary episodes. So long as jealousy is regarded as virtuous, such episodes cause grave friction; but they do not do so where a less restrictive morality is accepted on both sides. Relations involving children should be permanent if possible, but should not necessarily on that account be exclusive. Where there is mutual freedom and no pecuniary motive, love is good; where these conditions fail, it may often be bad. It is because they fail so frequently in the conventional marriage that a morality which is positive rather than restrictive, based upon hope rather than fear, is compelled, if it is logical, to disagree with the received code in matters of sex. And there can be no excuse for allowing our children to be taught a morality which we ourselves believe to be pernicious.

Finally, the attitude displayed by parents and teachers towards sex should be scientific, not emotional or dogmatic. For example, when it is said of a mother speaking to her daughter; "Let her tell nature's plan, *in a spirit of reverence*"; and of a father instructing his son: "The father should, in a spirit of reverence, explain nature's plan for the starting of a new life"—such sayings may be passed over by the reader as embodying nothing questionable. But to my mind there should be no more occasion for "reverence" than in explaining the construction of a steam-engine. "Reverence" means a special tone of voice from which the boy or girl infers that there is some peculiar quality about sex. From this to prurience and indecency is only a step. We shall never secure decency in matters of sex until we cease to treat the subject as different from any other. It follows that we must not advance dogmas for which there is no evidence, and which most impartial students question, such as: "After maturity is reached the ideal social relationship of the sexes is *monogamous* wedlock, to which relationship both parties should live in absolute fidelity" (ib. p. 310). This proposition may or may not be true; at present there is certainly no evidence sufficient to *prove* it true. By teaching it as something unquestionable, we abandon the scientific attitude, and do what we can to inhibit rational thought upon a most important matter. So long as this dogmatism persists in teachers, it is not to be hoped that their pupils will apply reason to any question upon which they feel strongly. And the only alternative to reason is violence.

CHAPTER XIII

IN previous chapters, I have tried to give an outline of what can be done for the young child in the way of creating the habits which will give happiness and usefulness in later life. But I have not discussed the question whether parents are to give this training, or whether it is to be given in schools designed for the purpose. I think the arguments in favour of the nursery-school are quite overwhelming—not only for children whose parents are poor, ignorant, and overworked, but for all children, or, at the very least, for all children who live in towns. I believe that the children at Miss Margaret McMillan's nursery-school in Deptford get something better than any children of well-to-do parents can at present obtain. I should like to see the same system extended to all children, rich and poor alike. But before discussing any actual nursery-school, let us see what reasons there are for desiring such an institution.

To begin with, early childhood is of immeasurable importance both medically and psychologically. These two aspects are very closely intertwined. For example: fear will make a child breathe badly, and breathing badly will predispose it to a variety of diseases.[1] Such interrelations are so numerous that no one can hope to succeed with a child's character without some medical knowledge, or with its health without some psychology. In both directions, most of the knowledge required is very new, and much of it runs counter to time-honoured traditions. Take for example the question of discipline. The great principle in a contest with a child is: do not yield, but do not punish. The normal parent sometimes yields for the sake of a quiet life, and sometimes punishes from exasperation; the right method, to be successful, requires a difficult combination of patience and power of suggestion. This is a psychological example; fresh air is a medical example. Given care and wisdom, children profit by constant fresh air, day and night, with not too much clothing. But if care and wisdom are absent, the risk of chills from wet or sudden cold cannot be ignored.

Parents cannot be expected to possess the skill or the leisure required for the new and difficult art of dealing with young children. In the case of uneducated parents, this is obvious; they do

---

[1] On this subject, *cf.* "The Nursery-School", by Margaret McMillan (Dent, 1919), p. 197.

not know the right methods, and if they were taught them they would remain unconvinced. I live in an agricultural district by the sea, where fresh food is easy to obtain, and there are no extremes of heat or cold; I chose it largely because it is ideal for children's health. Yet almost all the children of the farmers, shopkeepers, and so on, are pasty-faced languid creatures, because they are indulged in food and disciplined in play. They never go to the beach, because wet feet are thought dangerous. They wear thick woollen coats out-of-doors even in the hottest summer weather. If their play is noisy, steps are taken to make their behaviour "genteel". But they are allowed to stay up late, and are given all kinds of unwholesome tit-bits of grown-up food. Their parents cannot understand why my children have not died of cold and exposure long ago; but no object lesson will convince them that their own methods are capable of improvement. They are neither poor nor lacking in parental affection, but they are obstinately ignorant owing to bad education. In the case of town parents who are poor and overworked, the evils are of course far greater.

But even in the case of parents who are highly educated, conscientious, and not too busy, the children cannot get as much of what they need as in a nursery-school. First and foremost, they do not get the companionship of other children of the same age. If the family is small, as such families usually are, the children may easily get too much attention from their elders, and may become nervous and precocious in consequence. Moreover, parents cannot have the experience of multitudes of children which gives a sure touch. And only the rich can provide the space and the environment that best suits young children. Such things, if provided privately for one family of children, produce pride of possession and a feeling of superiority, which are extraordinarily harmful morally. For all these reasons, I belive that even the best parents would do well to send their children to a suitable school from the age of two onwards, at least for part of the day—provided such a school existed in their neighbourhood.

There are, at present, two kinds of schools, according to the status of the parents. There are Froebel schools and Montessori schools for well-to-do- children, and there are a small number of nursery schools for very poor children. Of the latter, the most famous is Miss McMillan's, of which the above-mentioned book gives an account which should be read by every lover of children. I am inclined to think that no existing school for well-to-do children is as good as hers, partly because she has larger numbers, partly because she is not troubled by the fussiness which middle-class snobbery obtrudes upon teachers. She aims at keeping children, if possible, from one year old till seven, though the education authorities incline to the view that the children ought to go to an ordinary elementary school at the age of five. The children come at eight in the morning, and stay till six in the evening; they have all their meals in the school. They spend as much as possible of their time out-of-doors, and indoors they have an abnormal amount of fresh air. Before a child is admitted, he or she is medically examined, and if possible cured at the clinic or in the hospital if not healthy. After admission, the children become and remain healthy with very few exceptions. There is a large, lovely garden, and a good deal of the time is spent in playing there. The teaching is broadly on Montessori lines. After dinner the children all sleep. In spite of the fact that at night, and on Sundays, they have to be in poverty-stricken homes, perhaps in cellars with drunken parents, their physique and intelligence become equal to the best that middle-class children achieve. Here is Miss McMillan's account of her seven-year-old pupils:

They are nearly all tall, straight children. All are straight, indeed, if not tall, but the average is a big, well-made child with clean skin, bright eyes, and silky hair. He or she is a little above the average of the best type of well-to-do child of the upper middle class. So much for his or her physique. Mentally he is alert, sociable, eager for life and new experience. He can read and spell perfectly, or almost perfectly. He writes well and expresses himself easily. He speaks good English and also French. He can not only help himself, but he or she has for years helped younger children: and he can count and measure and design and has had some preparation for science. His first years were spent in an atmosphere of love and calm and *fun*, and his last two years were full of interesting experiences and experiment. He knows about a garden, and has planted and watered, and taken care of plants as well as animals. The seven-year-old can dance, too, and sing and play many games. Such are the children who will soon present themselves in thousands at the Junior Schools' doors. What is to be done with them? I want to point out, first of all, that the elementary school teachers' work will be changed by this sudden uprush of clean and strong young life from below. Either the Nursery-School will be a paltry thing, that is to say a new failure, or else it will soon influence not only elementary schools but also the secondary. It will provide a new kind of children to be educated, and this must react sooner or later, not only on all the schools, but on all our social life, on the kind of government and laws framed for the people, and on the relation of our nation to other nations.

I do not think these claims exaggerated. The nursery-school, if it became universal, could, in one generation, remove the profound differences in education which at present divide the classes, could produce a population all enjoying the mental and physical development which is now confined to the most fortunate, and could remove the terrible dead-weight of disease and stupidity and malevolence which now makes progress so difficult. Under the Education Act of 1918, nursery-schools were to have been promoted by Government money; but when the Geddes Axe descended it was decided that it was more important to build cruisers and the Singapore Dock for the purpose of facilitating war with the Japanese. At the present moment, the Government is spending £650,000 a year to induce people to poison themselves with preservatives in Dominion butter and bacon rather than eat pure butter from Denmark. To secure this end, our children are condemned to disease and misery and unawakened intelligence, from which multitudes could be saved by £650,000 a year spent on nursery-schools. The mothers now have the vote; will they some day learn to use it for the good of their children? [2]

Apart from these wider considerations, what has to be realized is that the right care of young

[2] Although Miss McMillan is American, I understand that the importance of nursery-schools is even less appreciated in America than in England. As, however, there are not the financial difficulties which exist in Europe, it may be hoped that the movement will soon become widespread in the United States. There is no mention of it in O'Shea's book, though the need of it is evident from his remarks on p. 182.

children is highly skilled work, which parents cannot hope to do satisfactorily, and that it is quite different work from school-teaching in later years. To quote Miss McMillan again:

The Nursery child has a fairly good physique. Not only do his neighbours in the slums fall far short of him: his "betters" in good districts, the middle-class children, of a very good type, fall short of him. It is clear that something more than parental love and "parental responsibility" are wanted. Rules of thumb have all broken down. "Parental love" without knowledge has broken down. Child nurture has not broken down. It is very highly skilled work.

As regards the finances:

A Nursery-School of 100 children can be run to-day at an annual cost of £12 per head, and of this sum the parents in the poorest quarters can pay one-third. A Nursery-School staffed by students will cost more, but the greater part of the increased cost would be paid as fees and maintenance of future teachers. An open-air nursery and training centre, numbering in all about 100 children and thirty students, costs as nearly as makes no difference £2,200 per annum.

One more quotation:

One great result of the Nursery-School will be that the children can get faster through the curriculum of to-day. When they are half or two-thirds through the present elementary school life they will be ready to go on to more advanced work. . . . In short, the Nursery-School, if it is a *real* place of nurture, and not merely a place where babies are "minded" till they are five, will affect our whole educational system very powerfully and very rapidly. It will quickly raise the possible level of culture and attainment in all schools, beginning with the junior schools. It will prove that this welter of disease and misery in which we live, and which makes the doctor's service loom bigger than the teacher's, can be swept away. It will make the heavy walls, the terrible gates, the hard playground, the sunless and huge class-room look monstrous, as they are. It will give teachers a chance.

The nursery-school occupies an intermediate position between early training of character and subsequent giving of instruction. It carries on both at once, and each by the help of the other, with instruction gradually taking a larger share as the child grows older. It was in institutions having a similar function that Madame Montessori perfected her methods. In certain large tenement houses in Rome, a large room was set apart for the children between three and seven, and Madame Montessori was put in charge of these "Children's Houses".[3] As in Deptford, the children came from the very poorest section of the population; as in Deptford, the results showed that early

[3] See Montessori, "The Montessori Method" (Heinemann, 1912), p. 42 ff.

care can overcome the physical and mental disadvantages of a bad home.

It is remarkable that, ever since the time of Séguin, progress in educational methods with young children has come from study of idiots and the feeble-minded, who are, in certain respects, still mentally infants. I believe the reason for the necessity of this detour was that the stupidities of mental patients were not regarded as blameworthy, or as curable by chastisement; no one thought that Dr. Arnold's recipe of flogging would cure their "laziness". Consequently they were treated scientifically, not angrily; if they failed to understand, no irate pedagogue stormed at them and told them they ought to be ashamed of themselves. If people could have brought themselves to take a scientific instead of a moralizing attitude towards children, they could have discovered what is now known about the way to educate them without first having to study the mentally deficient. The conception of "moral responsibility" is "responsible" for much evil. Imagine two children, one of whom has the good fortune to be in a nursery-school, while the other is left to unalleviated slum-life. Is the second child "morally responsible" if he grows up less admirable than the first? Are his parents "morally responsible" for the ignorance and carelessness which makes them unable to educate him?   Are the rich "morally responsible" for the selfishness and stupidity which have been drilled into them at expensive schools, and which make them prefer their own foolish luxuries to the creation of a happy community? All are victims of circumstances; all have had characters warped in infancy and intelligence stunted at school.   No good purpose is served by choosing to regard them as "morally responsible", and holding them up to reprobation because they have been less fortunate than they might have been.

There is only one road to progress, in education as in other human affairs, and that is: Science wielded by love.   Without science, love is powerless; without love, science is destructive.   All that has been done to improve the education of little children has been done by those who loved them; all has been done by those who knew all that science could teach on the subject.   This is one of the benefits we derive from the higher education of women: in former days, science and love of children were much less likely to coexist.   The power of moulding young minds which science is placing in our possession is a very terrible power, capable of deadly misuse; if it falls into the wrong hands, it may produce a world even more ruthless and cruel than the haphazard world of nature. Children may be taught to be bigoted, bellicose, and brutal, under the pretence that they are being taught religion, patriotism, and courage, or communism, proletarianism, and revolutionary ardour. The teaching must be inspired by love, and must aim at creating love in the children. If not, it will become more efficiently harmful with every improvement in scientific technique. Love for children exists in the community as an effective force; this is shown by the lowering of the infant death-rate and the improvement of education. It is still far too weak, or our politicians would not dare to sacrifice the life and happiness of innumerable children to their nefarious schemes of bloodshed and oppression; but it exists and is increasing. Other forms of love, however, are strangely lacking. The very individuals who lavish care on children cherish passions which expose those same children, in later life, to death in wars which are mere collective insanities. Is it too much to hope that love may gradually be extended from the child to the man he will become? Will the lovers of children learn to follow their later years with something of the same parental solicitude? Having given them strong bodies and vigorous minds, shall we let them use their strength and vigour to create a better world? Or, when they turn to this work, shall we recoil in terror, and plunge

them back into slavery and drill?   Science is
ready for either alternative; the choice is between love and hate, though hate is disguised
beneath all the fine phrases to which professional moralists do homage.

PART III

INTELLECTUAL EDUCATION

CHAPTER XIV

GENERAL PRINCIPLES

THE building up of character, which has been our theme hitherto, should be mainly a matter for the earlier years. If rightly conducted, it ought to be nearly complete by the age of six. I do not mean that a character cannot be spoilt after that age; there is no age at which untoward circumstances or environment will not do harm. What I mean is that, after the age of six, a boy or girl who has been given the right early training ought to have habits and desires which will lead in the right direction if a certain care is taken with the environment. A school composed of boys and girls rightly brought up during their first six years will constitute a good environment, given a modicum of good sense in the authorities; it ought not to be necessary to give much time or thought to moral questions, since such further virtues as are required ought to result naturally from purely intellectual training. I do not mean to assert this pedantically as an absolute rule, but as a principle guiding school authorities as regards the matters upon which they ought to lay emphasis. I am convinced that, if children up to the age of six have been properly handled, it is best that the school authorities should lay stress upon purely intellectual progress, and should rely upon this to produce the further development of character which is still desirable.

It is a bad thing for intelligence, and ultimately for character, to let instruction be influenced by moral considerations. It should not be thought that some knowledge is harmful and some ignorance is good. The knowledge which is imparted should be imparted for an intellectual purpose, not to prove some moral or political conclusion. The purpose of the teaching should be, from the pupil's point of view, partly to satisfy his curiosity, partly to give him the skill required in order that he may be able to satisfy his curiosity for himself. From the teacher's point of view, there must also be the stimulation of certain fruitful kinds of curiosity. But there must never be discouragement of curiosity, even if it takes directions which lie outside the school curriculum altogether. I do not mean that the curriculum should be interrupted, but that the curiosity should be regarded as laudable, and the boy or girl should be told how to satisfy it after school hours, by means of books in the library for example.

But at this point I shall be met by an argument which must be faced at the outset. What if a boy's curiosity is morbid or perverted? What if he is interested in obscenity or in accounts of tortures? What if he is only interested in prying into other people's doings? Are such forms of curiosity to be encouraged? In answering this question, we must make a distinction. Most emphatically, we are not to behave so that the boy's curiosity shall continue to be limited to these directions. But it does not follow that we are to make him feel wicked for wishing to know about such things, or that we are to struggle to keep knowledge of them away from him. Almost always, the whole attraction of such knowledge consists in the fact that it is forbidden; in a certain number of cases, it is connected with some pathological mental condition which needs medical treatment. But in no case is prohibition and moral horror the right treatment. As the commonest and most important case, let us take an interest in obscenity. I do not believe that such a thing could exist in a boy or girl to whom sex knowledge was just like any other knowledge. A boy who obtains possession of indecent pictures is proud of his skill in having done so, and of knowing what his less enterprising companions have failed to find out. If he had been told openly and decently all about sex, he would

feel no interest in such pictures. If, nevertheless, a boy were found to have such an interest,
I should have him treated by a doctor skilled in
these matters. The treatment should begin by
encouraging him to utter freely even his most
shocking thoughts, and should continue with a
flood of further information, growing gradually more technical and scientific, until the
whole matter bored him to extinction. When
he felt that there was nothing more to know,
and that what he did know was uninteresting,
he would be cured. The important point is
that the knowledge in itself is not bad, but only
the habit of brooding on one particular topic.
An obsession is not cured, at first, by violent
efforts to distract attention, but rather by a
plethora of the subject. Through this, the interest can be made scientific instead of morbid;
and when that has been achieved, it takes its
legitimate place among other interests, and
ceases to be an obsession. This, I am convinced,
is the right way to deal with a narrow and
morbid curiosity. Prohibition and moral horror
can only make it worse.

Although improvement of character should
not be the aim of instruction, there are certain
qualities which are very desirable, and which
are essential to the successful pursuit of knowledge; they may be called the intellectual virtues. These should result from intellectual

education; but they should result as needed in learning, not as virtues pursued for their own sakes. Among such qualities the chief seem to me: curiosity, open-mindedness, belief that knowledge is possible though difficult, patience, industry, concentration and exactness. Of these, curiosity is fundamental; where it is strong and directed to the right objects, all the rest will follow. But perhaps curiosity is not quite so active as to be made the basis of the whole intellectual life. There should always also be a desire to *do* something difficult; the knowledge which is acquired should appear in the pupil's mind as skill, just like skill in games or gymnastics. It is, I suppose, unavoidable that the skill should be in part merely that required for artificial school tasks; but wherever it can be made to appear necessary for some non-scholastic purpose which appeals to the pupil, something very important has been accomplished. The divorce of knowledge from life is regrettable, although, during school years, it is not wholly avoidable. Where it is hardest to avoid, there should be occasional talks about the utility of the knowledge in question—taking "utility" in a very broad sense. Nevertheless, I should allow a large place to pure curiosity, without which much of the most valuable knowledge (for instance, pure mathematics) would never have been discovered. There is much knowledge which seems to me valuable on its own account, quite apart from any use to which it is capable of being put. And I should not wish to encourage the young to look too closely for an ulterior purpose in all knowledge; disinterested curiosity is natural to the young, and is a very valuable quality. It is only where it fails that I should appeal to the desire for skill such as can be exhibited in practice. Each motive has its place, but neither should be allowed to push the other aside.

I am aware that I have been assuming that some knowledge is desirable on its own account, not merely on account of its utility. This view is often challenged. I find it said by Professor O'Shea [1] that in European and Oriental schools "a person is not regarded as educated, or at least not cultured, unless he has amassed a considerable body of knowledge of ancient flavour. But in our country we are rapidly coming to the view that culture does not depend upon the mere possession of facts, whether ancient or modern. The cultured individual is one who has acquired knowledge and skill which make him of service to society, and habits of conduct which make him agreeable in association with his fellows. [2] Knowledge which does not function in the life of the individual in his relations

[1] O'Shea, p. 386.

[2] Are we to infer that culture consists in carrying a hip-flask? The definition seems applicable.

with others, to-day is not regarded by American teachers as of value for culture any more than for disciplinary purposes."

Of course this account of how the Old World regards culture is a caricature. No one would maintain that *mere* knowledge of facts confers culture. But it would be argued that culture implies a certain freedom from parochialism, both in space and time, and that this involves a respect for excellence even if it is found in another country or another age. We are apt to exaggerate our superiority not only to foreigners, but to the men of former times, and this makes us contemptuous of everything in which they were better than we are, which includes the whole æsthetic side of life. And I should say that culture involves a certain power of contemplation, for thinking or feeling without rushing headlong into energetic action. This leads me to a certain hesitation in adopting the theory of what is called "dynamic" education, which "requires pupils actually to *do* what they are learning" (ib. p. 401). Undoubtedly this method is right with young children, but education is not complete until more abstract and intellectual methods have become possible. To "do" the nebular hypothesis or the French Revolution would take a long time, not to mention danger from the guillotine. A person who has been adequately educated has learned to extract the meaning from abstractions when necessary, and to manipulate them as abstractions so long as that will serve his purpose. A mathematician who had to stop to realize the meaning of each step in his transformations would never get through his work; the essential merit of his instrument is that it can be used without this labour. In higher education, therefore, the dynamic method seems inadequate. I cannot help thinking that its popularity in America is partly due to the notion that all excellence consists in doing, rather than in thinking and feeling. This notion is implicit in the definition of culture which I quoted just now, and is natural in a mechanical age, since a machine can only do, and is not expected to think or feel. But the assimilation of men to machines, whatever may be thought of it metaphysically, is hardly likely to give us a just standard of values.

Open-mindedness is a quality which will always exist where desire for knowledge is genuine. It only fails where other desires have become entangled with the belief that we already know the truth. That is why it is so much commoner in youth than in later life. A man's activities are almost necessarily bound up with some decision on an intellectually doubtful matter. A clergyman cannot be disinterested about theology, nor a soldier about war. A lawyer is bound to hold that criminals ought to be punished—unless they can afford a leading lawyer's fee. A schoolmaster will favour the particular system of education for which he is fitted by his training and experience. A politician can hardly help believing in the principles of the party which is most likely to give him office. When once a man has chosen his career, he cannot be expected to be perpetually considering whether some other choice might not have been better. In later life, therefore, open-mindedness has its limitations, though they ought to be as few as possible. But in youth there are far fewer of what William James called "forced options", and therefore there is less occasion for the "will to believe". Young people ought to be encouraged to regard every question as open, and to be able to throw over any opinion as the result of an argument. It is implied in this freedom of thought that there should not be complete freedom of action. A boy must not be free to run off to sea under the influence of some story of adventure in the Spanish Main. But so long as his education continues, he should be free to *think* that it is better to be a pirate than a professor.

Power of concentration is a very valuable quality, which few people acquire except through education. It is true that it grows naturally, to a considerable extent, as young people get older; very young infants seldom think of any one thing for more than a few minutes, but with every year that passes their attention grows less volatile until they are adult. Nevertheless, they are hardly likely to acquire enough concentration without a long period of intellectual education. There are three qualities which distinguish perfect concentration: it should be intense, prolonged, and voluntary. Intensity is illustrated by the story of Archimedes, who is said to have never noticed when the Romans captured Syracuse and came to kill him, because he was absorbed in a mathematical problem. To be able to concentrate on the same matter for a considerable time is essential to difficult achievement, and even to the understanding of any complicated or abstruse subject. A profound spontaneous interest brings this about naturally, so far as the object of interest is concerned. Most people can concentrate on a mechanical puzzle for a long time; but this is not in itself very useful. To be really valuable, the concentration must also be within the control of the will. By this I mean that, even where some piece of knowledge is uninteresting in itself, a man can force himself to acquire it if he has an adequate motive for doing so. I think it is above all the control of attention by the will that is conferred by higher education. In this one respect, an old-fashioned education is admirable; I doubt whether modern methods are as successful in teaching a man to endure voluntary boredom. However, if this defect does exist in modern educational practice, it is by no means irremediable. The matter is one to which I shall return later.

Patience and industry ought to result from a good education. It was formerly thought that they could only be secured, in most cases, by the enforcement of good habits imposed by external authority. Undoubtedly this method has some success, as may be seen when a horse is broken in. But I think it is better to stimulate the ambition required for overcoming difficulties, which can be done by grading the difficulties so that the pleasure of success may at first be won fairly easily. This gives experience of the rewards of persistence, and gradually the amount of persistence required can be increased. Exactly similar remarks apply to the belief that knowledge is difficult but not impossible, which is best generated by inducing the pupil to solve a series of carefully graded problems.

Exactness, like the voluntary control of attention, is a matter to which educational reformers perhaps tend to attach too little importance. Dr. Ballard (*op. cit.* Chap. XVI) states definitely that our elementary schools, in this respect, are not so good as they were, although in most respects they are vastly improved. He says: "There is in existence a large number of tests given to school children in the annual examinations of the 'eighties and early 'nineties, and the results of those tests were scheduled for purposes of grant.[3] When those same tests are set to-day to children of the same age the results are palpably and consistently worse. Account for it as we may, there can be no doubt whatever about the fact. Taken as a whole, the work done in our schools—our primary schools at least—is less accurate than it was a quarter of a century ago." Dr. Ballard's whole discussion of this subject is so excellent that I have little to add to it. I will, however, quote his concluding words: "After all deductions have been made, it [accuracy] is still a noble and inspiring ideal. It is the morality of the intellect: it prescribes what it ought to strive for in the pursuit of its own proper ideal. For the extent to which we are accurate in our thoughts, words, and deeds is a rough measure of our fealty to truth."

The difficulty which is felt by the advocate of modern methods is that accuracy, as hitherto taught, involves boredom, and that it is an immense gain if education can be made interesting. Here, however, we must make a distinction.

---

[3] In those days, in England, the State bore only part of the expense of the school; this part was called a "grant", and depended upon the success of the children in examinations.

Boredom merely imposed by the teacher is wholly bad; boredom voluntarily endured by the pupil in order to satisfy some ambition is valuable if not overdone. It should be part of education to fire pupils with desires not easily gratified—to know the calculus, to read Homer, to perform well on the violin, or what not. Each of these involves its own kind of accuracy. Able boys and girls will go through endless tedium and submit willingly to severe discipline in order to acquire some coveted knowledge or skill. Those who have less native ability can often be fired by similar ambitions if they are inspiringly taught. The driving force in education should be the pupil's wish to learn, not the master's authority; but it does not follow that education should be soft and easy and pleasant at every stage. This applies, in particular, to the question of accuracy. The acquisition of exact knowledge is apt to be wearisome, but it is essential to every kind of excellence, and this fact can be made obvious to a child by suitable methods. In so far as modern methods fail in this respect, they are at fault. In this matter, as in many others, reaction against the old bad forms of discipline has tended to an undue laxity, which will have to give place to a new discipline, more internal and psychological than the old external authority. Of this new discipline, accuracy will be the intellectual expression.

There are various kinds of accuracy, each of which has its own importance. To take the main kinds: There is muscular accuracy, æsthetic accuracy, accuracy as to matter of fact, and logical accuracy. Every boy or girl can appreciate the importance of muscular accuracy in many directions; it is required for the control of the body which a healthy childs spends all its spare time in acquiring, and afterwards for the games upon which prestige depends. But it has other forms which have more to do with school teaching, such as well-articulated speech, good writing, and correct performance on a musical instrument. A child will think these things important or unimportant according to his environment. Æsthetic accuracy is difficult to define; it has to do with the appropriateness of a sensible stimulus for the production of emotion. One way of teaching an important form of it is to cause children to learn poetry by heart—*e. g.*, Shakespeare, for purposes of acting—and to make them feel, when they make mistakes, why the original is better. I believe it would be found that, where æsthetic sensibility is wide-spread, children are taught conventional stereotyped performances, such as dances and songs, which they enjoy, but which must be done exactly right on account of tradition. This makes them sensitive to small differences, which is essential to accuracy. Acting, singing, and dancing seem to me the best methods of teaching æsthetic precision. Drawing is less good, because it is likely to be judged by its fidelity to the model, not by æsthetic standards. It is true that stereotyped performances also are expected to reproduce a model, but it is a model created by æsthetic motives; it is copied because it is good, not because copying is good.

Accuracy as to matter of fact is intolerably boring when pursued on its own account. Learning the dates of the kings of England, or the names of the counties and their capitals, used to be one of the terrors of childhood. It is better to secure accuracy by interest and repetition. I could never remember the list of capes, but at eight years old I knew almost all the stations on the Underground. If children were shown a cinema representing a ship sailing round the coast, they would soon know the capes. I don't think they are worth knowing, but if they were, that would be the way to teach them. All geography ought to be taught on the cinema; so ought history at first. The initial expense would be great, but not too great for governments. And there would be a subsequent economy in ease of teaching.

Logical accuracy is a late acquisition, and should not be forced upon young children. Getting the multiplication table right is, of course, accuracy as to matter of fact; it only becomes logical accuracy at a much later stage. Mathematics is the natural vehicle for this teaching, but it fails if allowed to appear as a set of arbitrary rules. Rules must be learnt, but at some stage the reasons for them must be made clear; if this is not done, mathematics has little educative value.

I come now to a question which has already arisen in connection with exactness, the question, namely, how far it is possible or desirable to make all instruction interesting. The old view was that a great deal of it must be dull, and that only stern authority will induce the average boy to persist. (The average girl was to remain ignorant.) The modern view is that it can be made delightful through and through. I have much more sympathy with the modern view than with the old one; nevertheless, I think it is subject to some limitations, especially in higher education. I shall begin with what I think true in it.

Modern writers on infant psychology all emphasize the importance of not urging a young child to eat or sleep: these things ought to be done spontaneously by the child, not as a result of coaxing or forcing. My own experience entirely bears out this teaching. At first, we did not know the newer teaching, and tried the older methods. They were very unsuccessful, whereas the modern methods succeeded perfectly. It must not be supposed, however, that the modern parent does nothing about eating and sleeping; on the contrary, everything possible is done to promote the formation of good habits. Meals come at regular times, and the child must sit through them without games whether he eats or not. Bed comes at regular times, and the child must lie down in bed. He may have a toy animal to hug, but not one that squeaks or runs or does anything exciting. If the animal is a favourite, one may play the game that the animal is tired and the child must put it to sleep. Then leave the child alone, and sleep will usually come very quickly. But never let the child think you are anxious he should sleep or eat. That at once makes him think you are asking a favour; this gives him a sense of power, which leads him to demand more and more coaxing or punishment. He should eat and sleep because he wants to, not to please you.

This psychology is obviously applicable in great measure to instruction. If you insist upon teaching a child, he will conclude that he is being asked to do something disagreeable to please you, and he will have a psychological resistance. If this exists at the start, it will perpetuate itself; at a later age, the desirability of getting through examinations may become

evident, and there will be work for that purpose, but none from sheer interest in knowledge.
If, on the contrary, you can first stimulate the
child's desire to know, and then, as a favour,
give him the knowledge he wants, the whole
situation is different. Very much less external
discipline is required, and attention is secured
without difficulty. To succeed in this method,
certain conditions are necessary, which Madame
Montessori successfully produces among the
very young. The tasks must be attractive and
not too difficult. There must, at first, be the
example of other children at a slightly more
advanced stage. There must be no other
obviously pleasant occupation open to the child
at the moment. There are a number of things
the child may do, and he works by himself at
whichever he prefers. Almost all children
are perfectly happy in this régime, and learn to
read and write without pressure before they are
five years old.

How far similar methods can advantageously
be applied to older children is a debatable question. As children grow older, they become re-
sponsive to more remote motives, and it is no
longer necessary that every detail should be
interesting in itself. But I think the broad
principle that the impulse to education should
come from the pupil can be continued up to any
age. The environment should be such as to

stimulate the impulse, and to make boredom and isolation the alternative to learning. But any child that preferred this alternative on any occasion should be allowed to choose it. The principle of individual work can be extended, though a certain amount of class-work seems indispensable after the early years. But if external authority is necessary to induce a boy or girl to learn, unless there is a medical cause, the probability is that the teacher is at fault or that previous moral training has been bad. If a child has been properly trained up to the age of five or six, any good teacher ought to be able to win his interest at later stages.

If this is possible, the advantages are immense. The teacher appears as the friend of the pupil, not as his enemy. The child learns faster, because he is co-operating. He learns with less fatigue, because there is not the constant strain of bringing back a reluctant and bored attention. And his sense of personal initiative is cultivated instead of being diminished. On account of these advantages, it seems worth while to assume that the pupil can be led to learn by the force of his own desires, without the exercise of compulsion by the teacher. If, in a small percentage of cases, the method were found to be a failure, these cases could be isolated and instructed by different methods. But I believe that, given methods adapted to the child's intelligence, there would be very few failures.

For reasons already given in connection with accuracy, I do not believe that a really thorough education can be made interesting through and through. However much one may wish to know a subject, some parts of it are sure to be found dull. But I believe that, given suitable guidance, a boy or girl can be made to feel the importance of learning the dull parts, and can be got through them also without compulsion. I should use the stimulus of praise and blame, applied as the result of good or bad performance of set tasks. Whether a pupil possesses the necessary skill should be made as obvious as in games or gymnastics. And the importance of the dull parts of a subject should be made clear by the teacher. If all these methods failed, the child would have to be classified as stupid, and taught separately from children of normal intelligence, though care must be taken not to let this appear as a punishment.

Except in very rare cases, the teacher, even at an early age (*i.e.*, after four, say) should not be either parent. Teaching is work requiring a special type of skill, which can be learnt, but which most parents have not had the opportunity of learning. The earlier the age of the pupil, the greater is the pedagogical skill required. And apart from this, the parent has been in constant contact with the child before formal education began, so that the child has a set of habits and expectations towards the parent which are not quite appropriate towards a teacher. The parent, moreover, is likely to be too eager and too much interested in his child's progress. He will be inordinately pleased by the child's cleverness and exasperated by his stupidity. There are the same reasons for not teaching one's own children as have led medical men not to treat their own families. But of course I do not mean that parents should not give such instruction as comes naturally; I mean only that they are, as a rule, not the best people for formal school lessons, even when they are well qualified to teach other people's children.

Throughout education, from the first day to the last, there should be a sense of intellectual adventure. The world is full of puzzling things which can be understood by sufficient effort. The sense of understanding what had been puzzling is exhilarating and delightful; every good teacher should be able to give it. Madame Montessori describes the delight of her children when they find they can write; I remember a sense almost of intoxication when I first read Newton's deduction of Kepler's Second Law from the law of gravitation. Few joys are so pure or so useful as this. Initiative and individual work give the pupil the opportunity of discovery, and thus afford the sense of mental adventure far more often and more keenly than is possible where everything is taught in class. Wherever it is possible, let the student be active rather than passive. This is one of the secrets of making education a happiness rather than a torment.

CHAPTER XV

THE questions: what should be taught? and how should it be taught? are intimately connected, because, if better methods of teaching are devised, it is possible to learn more. In particular, more can be learnt if the pupils wish to learn than if they regard work as a bore. I have already said something about methods, and I shall say more in a later chapter. For the present, I shall assume that the best possible methods are employed, and I shall consider what ought to be taught.

When we consider what an adult ought to know, we soon realize that there are things which everybody ought to know, and other things which it is necessary that some should know, though others need not. Some must know medicine, but for the bulk of mankind it is sufficient to have an elementary knowledge of physiology and hygiene. Some must know higher mathematics, but the bare elements suffice for those to whom mathematics is distasteful. Some should know how to play the trombone, but mercifully it is not necessary that every school-child should practise this instrument. In the main, the things taught at school before the age of fourteen should be among those that every one ought to know; apart from exceptional cases, specialization ought to come later. It should, however, be one of the aims of education before fourteen to discover special aptitudes in boys and girls, so that, where they exist, they may be carefully developed in the later years. For this reason, it is well that everybody should learn the bare beginnings of subjects which need not be further pursued by those who are bad at them.

When we have decided what every adult ought to know, we have to decide the order in which subjects are to be taught; here we shall naturally be guided by relative difficulty, teaching the easiest subjects first. To a great extent, these two principles determine the curriculum in the early school years.

I shall assume that, by the time a child is five years old, he knows how to read and write. This should be the business of the Montessori school, or whatever improvement upon it may hereafter be devised. There, also, the child learns a certain accuracy in sense-perception, the rudiments of drawing and singing and dancing, and the power to concentrate upon some educational occupation in the middle of a number of other children. Of course the child will not be very perfect in these respects at five years old, and will need further teaching in all of them for some years to come. I do not think that anything involving severe mental effort should be undertaken before the age of seven, but by sufficient skill difficulties can be enormously diminished. Arithmetic is a bugbear of childhood—I remember weeping bitterly because I could not learn the multiplication table —but if it is tackled gradually and carefully, as it is by means of the Montessori apparatus, there is no need of the sense of blank despair which its mysteries used to inspire. In the end, however, there must be a good deal of rather tiresome mastering of rules if sufficient facility is to be acquired. This is the most awkward of early school subjects to fit into a curriculum intended to be interesting; nevertheless, a certain degree of proficiency is necessary for practical reasons. Also, arithmetic affords the natural introduction to accuracy: the answer to a sum is either right or wrong, and never "interesting" or "suggestive". This makes arithmetic important as one element in early education, quite apart from its practical utility. But its difficulties should be carefully graded and spread out thin; not too much time at a stretch should be devoted to them.

Geography and history were, when I was young, among the worst taught of all subjects. I dreaded the geography lesson, and if I tolerated the history lesson it was only because I have always had a passion for history. Both subjects might be made fascinating to quite young children. My little boy, though he has never had a lesson, already knows far more geography than his nurse. He has acquired his knowledge through the love of trains and steamers which he shares with all boys. He wants to know of journeys that his imaginary steamers are to make, and he listens with the closest attention while I tell him the stages of the journey to China. Then, if he wishes it, I show him pictures of the various countries on the way. Sometimes he insists upon pulling out the big Atlas and looking at the journey on the map. The journey between London and Cornwall in the train, which he makes twice a year, interests him passionately, and he knows all the stations where the train stops or where carriages are slipped. He is fascinated by the North Pole and the South Pole, and puzzled because there is no East Pole or West Pole. He knows the directions of France and Spain and America over the sea, and a good deal about what is to be seen in those countries. None of this has come by way of instruction, but all in response to an eager curiosity. Almost every child becomes interested in geography as soon as it is associated with the idea of travel. I should teach geography partly by pictures and tales about travellers, but mainly by the cinema, showing what the traveller sees on his journey. The knowledge of geographical facts is useful, but without intrinsic intellectual value; when, however, geography is made vivid by pictures, it has the merit of giving food for imagination. It is good to know that there are hot countries and cold countries, flat countries and mountainous countries, black men, yellow men, brown men, and red men, as well as white men. This kind of knowledge diminishes the tyranny of familiar surroundings over the imagination, and makes it possible in later life to *feel* that distant countries really exist, which otherwise is very difficult except by travelling. For these reasons, I should give geography a large place in the teaching of very young children, and I should be astonished if they did not enjoy the subject. Later on, I should give them books with pictures, maps, and elementary information about different parts of the world, and get them to put together little essays about the peculiarities of various countries.

What applies to geography applies even more strongly to history, though at a slightly more

advanced age, because the sense of time is rudi-
mentary at first. I think history can profitably
be begun at about five years old, at first with
interesting stories of eminent men, abundantly
illustrated. I myself had, at that age, a pic-
ture-history of England. Queen Matilda cross-
ing the Thames at Abingdon on the ice made
such a profound impression upon me that I
still felt thrilled when I did the same thing
at the age of eighteen, and quite imagined that
King Stephen was after me. I believe hardly
any boy of five years old would fail to be interested by the life of Alexander. Columbus
perhaps belongs more to geography than to history; I can testify that he becomes interesting
before the age of two, at least to children who
know the sea. By the time a child is six years
old, he ought to be ripe for an outline of world-
history, treated more or less on Mr. Wells's or
Mr. Van Loon's lines, with the necessary sim-
plifications, and with pictures, or the cinema if
possible. If he lives in London, he can see the
strange beasts in the Natural History Museum;
but I should not take him to the British Museum before the age of ten or thereabouts. It is
necessary to be careful, in teaching history, not
to obtrude aspects which are interesting to
us until the child is ripe for them. The two
aspects which are first interesting are: the gen-

eral pageant and procession, from geology to man, from savage man to civilized man, and so on; and the dramatic story-telling interest of incidents which have a sympathetic hero. But I think we should keep in our own minds, as a guiding thread, the conception of gradual chequered progress, perpetually hampered by the savagery which we inherit from the brutes, and yet gradually leading on towards mastery of ourselves and our environment through knowledge. The conception is that of the human race as a whole, fighting against chaos without and darkness within, the little tiny lamp of reason growing gradually into a great light by which the night is dispelled. The divisions between races, nations and creeds should be treated as follies, distracting us in the battle against Chaos and Old Night, which is our one truly human activity.

I should give first the illustrations of this theme, and only afterwards, if ever, the theme itself. I should show savage man cowering in the cold, gnawing the raw fruits of the earth. I should show the discovery of fire, and its effects; in this connection, the story of Prometheus would be in place. I should show the beginnings of agriculture in the Nile Valley, and the domestication of sheep and cows and dogs. I should show the growth of ships from

canoes to the largest liners, and the growth of
cities from colonies of cave-dwellers to London
and New York. I should show the gradual
growth of writing and of numerals. I should
show the brief gleam of Greece, the diffused
magnificence of Rome, the subsequent darkness, and the coming of science. The whole
of this could be made interesting in detail
even to very young children. I should not
keep silence about wars and persecutions and
cruelties, but I should not hold up military conquerors to admiration. The true
conquerors, in my teaching of history, should
be those who did something to dispel the darkness within and without—Buddha and Socrates,
Archimedes, Galileo and Newton, and all the
men who have helped to give us mastery over
ourselves or over nature. And so I should build
up the conception of a lordly splendid destiny
for the human race, to which we are false when
we revert to wars and other atavistic follies, and
true only when we put into the world something
that adds to our human dominion.

In the early years at school, there should be a
time set apart for dancing, which is good for
the body and a training for the æsthetic sense,
besides being a great pleasure to the children.
Collective dances should be taught after the
elements have been learnt; this is a form of

co-operation which young children easily appreciate. Similar remarks apply to singing, though it should begin a little later than dancing, both because it does not afford the same muscular delight, and because its rudiments are more difficult. Most children, though not all, will enjoy singing, and after nursery rhymes they should learn really beautiful songs. There is no reason to corrupt their taste first and try to purify it afterwards. At the best, this makes people precious. Children, like adults, differ enormously in musical capacity, so that the more difficult singing classes would have to be reserved for a selection among the older children. And among them singing ought to be voluntary, not enforced.

The teaching of literature is a matter as to which it is easy to make mistakes. There is not the slightest use, either for young or old, in being well-informed *about* literature, knowing the dates of the poets, the names of their works, and so on. Everything that can be put into a handbook is worthless. What is valuable is great familiarity with certain examples of good literature—such familiarity as will influence the style, not only of writing, but of thought. In old days the Bible supplied this to English children, certainly with a beneficial effect upon prose style; but few modern children know the

Bible intimately. I think the good effect of literature cannot be fully obtained without learning by heart. This practice used to be advocated as a training for the memory, but psychologists have shown that it has little, if any, effect in this way. Modern educationists give it less and less place. But I think they are mistaken, not because of any possible improvement of memory, but on account of the effect upon beauty of language in speech and writing. This should come without effort, as a spontaneous expression of thought; but in order to do so, in a community which has lost the primitive æsthetic impulses, it is necessary to produce a habit of thought which I believe is only to be generated by intimate knowledge of good literature. That is why learning by heart seems to me important.

But mere learning of set pieces, such as "the quality of mercy" and "all the world's a stage", seems tedious and artificial to most children, and therefore fails of its purpose. It is much better that learning by heart should be associated with acting, because then it is a necessary means to something which every child loves. From the age of three onwards, children delight in acting a part; they do it spontaneously, but are over-joyed when more elaborate ways of doing it are put in their way. I remember the exquisite amusement with which I acted the quarrel scene between Brutus and Cassius, and declaimed:

> I had rather be a dog and bay the moon
> Than such a Roman.

Children who take part in performing *Julius Cæsar* or *The Merchant of Venice* or any other suitable play will not only know their own parts, but most of the other parts as well. The play will be in their thoughts for a long time, and all by way of enjoyment. After all, good literature is intended to give pleasure, and if children cannot be got to derive pleasure from it they are hardly likely to derive benefit either. For these reasons, I should confine the teaching of literature, in early years, to the learning of parts for acting. The rest should consist of voluntary reading of well-written stories, obtainable in the school library. People nowadays write silly sentimental stuff for children, which insults them by not taking them seriously. Contrast the intense seriousness of "Robinson Crusoe". Sentimentality, in dealing with children and elsewhere, is a failure of dramatic sympathy. No child thinks it charming to be childish; he wants, as soon as possible, to learn to behave like a grown-up person. Therefore a book for children ought never to display a patronizing pleasure in childish ways. The artificial silliness of many modern children's

books is disgusting.   It must either annoy a
child, or puzzle and confuse his impulse towards
mental growth.   For this reason, the best books
for children are those that happen to suit them,
though written for grown-up people.   The only
exceptions are books written for children but
delightful also to grown-up people, such as
Lear and Lewis Carroll.

The question of modern languages is one
which is not altogether easy.   In childhood it
is possible to learn to speak a modern language
perfectly, which can never be achieved in later
years; there are therefore strong grounds for
teaching languages at an early age, if at all.
Some people seem to fear that knowledge of
one's own language suffers if others are learnt
too soon.   I do not believe this.   Tolstoy and
Turgenev were quite competent in Russian,
though they learnt English, French and German in infancy.   Gibbon could write in French
as easily as in English, but this did not spoil his
English style.   All through the eighteenth
century, all English aristocrats learnt French
in early youth as a matter of course, and many
also learnt Italian; yet their English was vastly
better than that of their modern descendants.
A child's dramatic instinct prevents it from
confusing one language with another, provided
it speaks them to different people.   I learnt
German at the same time as English, and spoke

it to nurses and governesses up to the age of ten; then I learnt French, and spoke it to governesses and tutors. Neither language ever confused itself with English, because it had different personal associations. I think that if a modern language is to be taught, it should be taught by a person whose native language it is, not only because it will be better taught, but because children feel less artificiality in talking a foreign language to a foreigner than in talking it to a person whose natural language is the same as their own. I think, therefore, that every school for children ought to have a French mistress, and if possible a German mistress too, who should not formally instruct the children in her language, except quite at first, but should play games with them and talk to them, and make the success of the games depend upon their understanding and answering. She could start with *Frère Jacques* and *Sur le pont d'Avignon*, and go on gradually to more complicated games. In this way the language could be acquired without any mental fatigue, and with all the pleasure of play-acting. And it can be acquired then far more perfectly and with less waste of valuable educational time than at any subsequent period.

The teaching of mathematics and science can only be begun towards the end of the years that we are considering in this chapter—say at the age of twelve. Of course I assume that arithmetic has already been taught, and that there have been popular talks about astronomy and geology, about prehistoric animals, famous explorers, and such naturally interesting matters. But I am thinking now of formal teaching—geometry and algebra, physics and chemistry. A few boys and girls like geometry and algebra, but the great majority do not. I doubt if this is wholly due to faulty methods of teaching. A sense for mathematics, like musical capacity, is mainly a gift of the gods, and I believe it to be quite rare, even in a moderate degree. Nevertheless, every boy and girl should have a taste of mathematics, in order to discover those who have a talent for it. Also, even those who learn little profit by the knowledge that there is such a subject. And by good methods almost everybody can be made to understand the elements of geometry. Of algebra I cannot say the same; it is more abstract than geometry, and essentially unintelligible to those whose minds are incapable of detachment from the concrete. A taste for physics and chemistry, properly taught, would probably be found to be less rare than a taste for mathematics, though still existing only in a minority of young people. Both mathematics and science, in the years from twelve to fourteen, ought only to be pursued to the point at which it becomes clear whether a boy or girl has any aptitude for them. This, of course, is not immediately evident. I loathed algebra at first, although afterwards I had some facility in it. In some cases, it would still be doubtful at the age of fourteen whether there was ability or not. In these cases, tentative methods would have to be continued for a while. But in most cases a decision could be made at fourteen. Some would definitely like the subjects and be good at them, others would dislike them and be bad at them. It would very seldom happen that a clever pupil disliked them or a stupid pupil liked them.

What has been said about mathematics and science applies equally to the classics. Between twelve and fourteen, I should give just so much instruction in Latin as would suffice to show which boys and girls had a love of the subject and facility for it. I am assuming that at fourteen education should begin to be more or less specialized, according to the tastes and aptitudes of the pupil. The last years before this moment arrives should be spent in finding out what it will be best to teach in subsequent years.

All through the school years, education in outdoor things should continue. In the case of well-to-do children, this can be left to the parents, but with other children it will have to be partly the business of the school. When I speak of education in outdoor things, I am not thinking of games. They, of course, have their importance, which is sufficiently recognized; but I am thinking of something different: knowledge of agricultural processes, familiarity with animals and plants, gardening, habits of observation in the country, and so on. I have been amazed to discover that town-bred people seldom know the points of the compass, never know which way the sun goes round, cannot find out which side of the house is out of the wind, and are generally destitute of knowledge which every cow or sheep possesses. This is the result of life exclusively in towns. Perhaps I shall be thought fanciful if I say that it is one reason why the labour party cannot win rural constituencies. But it certainly is the reason why town-bred people are so utterly divorced from everything primitive and fundamental. It has to do with something trivial and superficial and frivolous in their attitude to life—not of course always, but very often. The seasons and the weather, sowing and harvest, crops and flocks and herds, have a certain human importance, and ought to be intimate and familiar to everybody if the divorce from mother earth is not to be too complete. All this knowledge can be acquired by children in the course of activities which are of immense value to health, and deserve to be undertaken for that reason alone. And the pleasure of town children in the country shows that a profound need is being satisfied. So long as it is not satisfied, our educational system is incomplete.

CHAPTER XVI

AFTER the summer holidays in the fifteenth year, I shall assume that a boy or girl who so desires is allowed to specialize, and that this will be done in a large proportion of cases. But where there is no definite preference, it will be better to prolong an all-round education. And in exceptional cases specializing may begin earlier. All rules, in education, should be capable of being broken for special reasons. But I think that, as a general rule, pupils of more than average intelligence should begin to specialize at about fourteen, while pupils of less than average intelligence should usually not specialize at all at school, unless in the way of vocational training. I am refraining, in this book, from saying anything on this subject. But I do not believe that it ought to begin before fourteen, and I do not think that, even then, it ought to take up the whole of the school time of any pupil. I do not propose to discuss how much time it should take up, or whether it should be given to all pupils or only to some.

These questions raise economic and political issues which are only indirectly connected with education, and which cannot be discussed briefly. I therefore confine myself to the scholastic education in the years after fourteen.

I should make three broad divisions in school: (1) classics, (2) mathematics and science, (3) modern humanities. This last should include modern languages, history, and literature. In each division it might be possible to specialize somewhat more before leaving school, which I shall suppose does not occur before eighteen. Obviously all who take classics must do both Latin and Greek, but some may do more of the one, and some more of the other. Mathematics and science should go together at first, but in some sciences it is possible to achieve eminence without much mathematics, and in fact many eminent men of science have been bad mathematicians. I should, therefore, at the age of sixteen, allow a boy or girl to specialize in science or to specialize in mathematics, without entirely neglecting the branch not chosen. Similar remarks apply to modern humanities.

Certain subjects, of great utilitarian importance, would have to be taught to everybody. Among these, I should include anatomy, physiology and hygiene, to the extent that is likely to be required in adult daily life. But perhaps these subjects ought to come at an earlier stage, since they are naturally connected with sex education, which ought to be given, as far as possible, before puberty. The objection to putting them very early is that they ought not to be forgotten before they are needed. I think the only solution is to give them twice over, once, very simply and in bare outline, before puberty, and again later in connection with elementary knowledge about health and disease. I should say that every pupil ought to know something also about Parliament and the Constitution, but care must be taken to prevent teaching on this subject from degenerating into political propaganda.

More important than the curriculum is the question of the methods of teaching and the spirit in which the teaching is given. As to this, the main problem is to make the work interesting without making it too easy. Exact and detailed study should be supplemented by books and lectures on general aspects of the studies concerned. Before sitting down to a Greek play, I would have the students read a translation, by Gilbert Murray or some other translator with a poetic gift. Mathematics should be diversified by an occasional lecture on the history of mathematical discovery, and on the influence of this or that piece of mathematics upon science and daily life, with hints of the delightful things to be found in higher mathematics. Similarly the detailed study of history should be supplemented by brilliant outlines, even if they contained questionable generalizations. The students might be told that the generalizations are doubtful, and be invited to consider their detailed knowledge as supporting or refuting them. In science, it is good to read popular books which give an *aperçu* of recent research, in order to have some idea of the general scientific purpose served by particular facts and laws. All these things are useful as incentives to exact and minute study, but are pernicious if they are treated as substitutes for it. Pupils must not be encouraged to think that there are short cuts to knowledge. This is a real danger in modern education, owing to the reaction against the old severe drill. The mental work involved in the drill was good; what was bad was the killing of intellectual interests. We must try to secure the hard work, but by other methods than those of the old disciplinarian. I do not believe this is impossible. One finds in America that men who were idle as undergraduates work hard in the law school or the medical school, because at last they are doing work which strikes them as important. That is the essence of the matter: make the school work seem important to the pupils, and they will work hard. But if you make the

work too easy, they will know, almost by instinct, that you are not giving them what is
really worth having. Clever boys and girls like
to test their minds on difficulties. With good
teaching and the elimination of fear, very many
boys and girls would be clever who now seem
stupid and lethargic.

All through education, initiative should come
from the pupil as far as possible. Madame
Montessori has shown how this can be done
with very young children, but with older children different methods are required. It is, I
think, generally recognized by progressive educationists that there should be much more individual work and much less class work than has
been customary, though the individual work
should be done in a room full of other boys
and girls similarly engaged. Libraries and
laboratories should be adequate and roomy. A
considerable part of the working day should be
set apart for voluntary self-directed study, but
the pupil should write an account of what he or
she is studying, with an abstract of any information acquired. This helps to fix things in the
memory, to make reading have a purpose instead of being desultory, and to give the teacher
just that amount of control which may be necessary in each case. The cleverer the pupil, the
less control is required. With those who are

not very clever it will be necessary to give a great deal of guidance; but even with them it should be by way of suggestion, inquiry, and stimulus rather than by command. There should, however, also be set themes, giving practice in ascertaining the facts about some prescribed subject, and in presenting them in an orderly manner.

In addition to regular work, boys and girls ought to be encouraged to take an interest in current controversial questions of importance, political, social, and even theological. They should be encouraged to read all sides in such controversies, not only the orthodox side. If any of them have strong feelings on one side or the other, they should be told how to find out facts which support their view, and should be set to debate with those who hold the opposite view. Debates, conducted seriously with a view to ascertaining the truth, could be of great value. In these, the teacher should learn not to take sides, even if he or she has strong convictions. If almost all the pupils take one side, the teacher should take the other, saying that it is only for purposes of argument. Otherwise, his part should be confined to correcting mistakes as to facts. By such means, the pupils could learn discussion as a means of ascertaining truth, not as a contest for rhetorical victory.

If I were at the head of a school for older boys and girls, I should consider it equally undesirable to shirk current questions and to do propaganda about them. It is a good thing to make pupils feel that their education is fitting them to cope with matters about which the world is excited; it gives them a sense that scholastic teaching is not divorced from the practical world. But I should not urge my own views upon the pupils. What I should do is to put before them the ideal of a scientific attitude to practical questions. I should expect them to produce arguments that are arguments, and facts that are facts. In politics, especially, this habit is as rare as it is valuable. Every vehement political party generates a cocoon of myth, within which its mentality peacefully slumbers. Passion, too often, kills intellect; in intellectuals, on the contrary, intellect not infrequently kills passion. My aim would be to avoid both these misfortunes. Passionate feeling is desirable, provided it is not destructive; intellect is desirable, with the same proviso. I should wish the fundamental political passions to be constructive, and I should try to make the intellect serve these passions. But it must serve them genuinely, objectively, not only in the world of dreams. When the real world is not sufficiently flattering we all tend to take refuge in an imaginary world, where our desires are gratified without great effort. This is the essence of hysteria. It is also the source of nationalist, theological, and class myths. It shows a weakness of character which is almost universal in the present world. To combat this weakness of character should be one of the aims of later school education. There are two ways of combating it, both necessary, though in a sense opposites. The one is to increase our sense of what we can achieve in the world of reality; the other is to make us more sensitive to what reality can do in the way of dispelling our dreams. Both are comprised in the principle of living objectively rather than subjectively.

The classic example of subjectivity is Don Quixote. The first time he made a helmet, he tested its capacity for resisting blows, and battered it out of shape; next time he did not test it, but "deemed" it to be a very good helmet. This habit of "deeming" dominated his life. But every refusal to face unpleasant facts is of the same kind: we are all Don Quixotes more or less. Don Quixote would not have done as he did if he had been taught at school to make a really good helmet, and if he had been surrounded by companions who refused to "deem" whatever he wished to believe. The habit of living in fancies is normal and right in early childhood, because young children have an impotence which is not pathological. But as adult life approaches, there must be a more and more vivid realization that dreams are only valuable in so far as they can be translated, sooner or later, into fact. Boys are admirable in correcting the purely personal claims of other boys; in a school, it is difficult to cherish illusions as to one's power in relation to schoolfellows. But the myth-making faculty remains active in other directions, often with the co-operation of the masters. One's own school is the best in the world; one's country is always right and always victorious; one's social class (if one is rich) is better than any other class. All these are undesirable myths. They lead us to deem that we have a good helmet, when in fact some one else's sword could cut it in two. In this way they promote laziness and lead ultimately to disaster.

To cure this habit of mind, it is necessary, as in many other cases, to replace fear by rational prevision of misfortune. Fear makes people unwilling to face real dangers. A person afflicted with subjectivity, if awakened in the middle of the night by the cry of "fire", might decide that it must be his neighbour's house, since the truth would be too terrifying; he might thus lose the moment when escape was still possible. This, of course, could only occur in a pathological case; but in politics the analogous behaviour is normal. Fear, as an emotion, is disastrous in all cases where the right course can only be discovered by thinking; we want, therefore, to be able to foresee possibilities of evil without feeling fear, and to use our intelligence for the purpose of avoiding what is not inevitable. Evils which are really inevitable have to be treated with sheer courage; but it is not of them that I am speaking.

I do not want to repeat what I said about fear in a former chapter; I am concerned with it now only in the intellectual sphere, as an obstacle to truthful thinking. In this sphere, it is much easier to overcome in youth than in later life, because a change of opinion is less likely to bring grave misfortune to a boy or girl than to an adult, whose life is built upon certain postulates. For this reason, I should encourage a habit of intelligent controversy among the older boys and girls, and I should place no obstacles in their way even if they questioned what I regarded as important truths. I should make it my object to teach thinking, not orthodoxy, or even heterodoxy. And I should absolutely never sacrifice intellect to the fancied interest of morals. It is generally held that the teaching of virtue demands the incul-

cation of falsehood.   In politics, we conceal the
vices of eminent statesmen of our own party.
In theology, we conceal the sins of Popes if we
are Catholics, and the sins of Luther and Calvin
if we are Protestants.   In matters of sex, we
pretend before young people that virtue is much
commoner than it is.   In all countries, even
adults are not allowed to know certain kinds of
facts which the police consider undesirable, and
the censor, in England, does not allow plays to
be true to life, since he holds that the public
can only be cajoled into virtue by deceit.   This
whole attitude implies a certain feebleness.   Let
us know the truth, whatever it is; then we can
act rationally.   The holders of power wish to
conceal the truth from their slaves, in order
that they may be misled as to their own interests; this is intelligible.   What is less intelligible is that democracies should voluntarily
make laws designed to prevent themselves from
knowing the truth.   This is collective Quixot-
ism: they are resolved not to be told that the
helmet is less good than they wish to believe.
Such an attitude of abject funk is unworthy of
free men and women.   In my school, no obstacle
to knowledge shall exist of any sort or kind.
I shall seek virtue by the right training of
passions and instincts, not by lying and deceit.
In the virtue that I desire, the pursuit of knowl-

edge, without fear and without limitation, is an essential element, in the absence of which the rest has little value.

What I am saying is no more than this: that I should cultivate the scientific spirit. Many eminent men of science do not have this spirit outside their special province; I should seek to make it all-pervasive. The scientific spirit demands in the first place a wish to find out the truth; the more ardent this wish, the better. It involves, in addition, certain intellectual qualities. There must be preliminary uncertainty, and subsequent decision according to the evidence. We must not imagine in advance that we already know what the evidence will prove. Nor must we be content with a lazy scepticism, which regards objective truth as unattainable and all evidence as inconclusive. We should admit that even our best-founded beliefs probably stand in need of *some* correction; but truth, so far as it is humanly attainable, is a matter of degree. Our beliefs in physics are certainly less false now than they were before the time of Galileo. Our beliefs as to child psychology are certainly nearer to the truth than Dr. Arnold's were. In each case, the advance has come through substituting observation for preconceptions and passions. It is for the sake of this step that preliminary uncertainty is so important.   It is necessary, therefore, to teach this, and also to teach the skill required for marshalling evidence.   In a world where rival propagandists are perpetually blazing falsehoods at us, to induce us to poison ourselves with pills or each other with poison gases, this critical habit of mind is enormously important.   Ready credulity in the face of repeated assertions is one of the curses of the modern world, and schools should do what they can to guard against it.

Throughout the later school years, even more than earlier, there should be a sense of intellectual adventure.   Pupils should be given the opportunity of finding out exciting things for themselves after their set tasks were done, and therefore the set tasks should not be too heavy. There must be praise whenever it is deserved, and although mistakes must be pointed out, it should be done without censure.   Pupils should never be made to feel ashamed of their stupidity.   The great stimulus in education is to feel that achievement is possible.   Knowledge which is felt to be boring is of little use, but knowledge which is assimilated eagerly becomes a permanent possession.   Let the relation of knowledge to real life be very visible to your pupils, and let them understand how by knowledge the world could be transformed.   Let the teacher appear always the ally of the pupil, not his natural enemy. Given a good training in the early years, these precepts will suffice to make the acquisition of knowledge delightful to the great majority of boys and girls.

CHAPTER XVII

WHETHER a boy or girl should be sent to a boarding school or a day school is, to my mind, a question which must be decided in each case according to circumstances and temperament. Each system has its own advantages; in some cases the advantages of one system are greater, in others those of the other. I propose, in this chapter, to set forth the kind of arguments which would weigh with me in deciding about my own children, and which, I imagine, would be likely to weigh with other conscientious parents.

There are first of all considerations of health. Whatever may be true of actual schools, it is clear that schools are capable of being made more scientifically careful in this respect than most homes, because they can employ doctors and dentists and matrons with the latest knowledge, whereas busy parents are likely to be comparatively uninformed medically. Moreover, schools can be put in healthy neighbourhoods. In the case of people who live in big towns, this argument alone is very powerful in favour of boarding schools. It is obviously better for young people to spend most of their life in the country, so that if their parents have to live in towns it may be desirable to send the children away for their schooling. This argument may perhaps cease, before long, to have much validity: the health of London, for example, is steadily improving, and might be brought up to the standard of the country by the artificial use of ultra-violet light. Nevertheless, even if illness could be brought as low as in the country, a considerable nervous strain would remain. Constant noise is bad for both children and adults; the sights of the country, the smell of damp earth, the wind and the stars, ought to be stored in the memory of every man and woman. I think, therefore, that life in the country for the greater part of the year will remain important for the young whatever improvements may be effected in urban health.

Another argument, though a much smaller one, in favour of boarding schools is that they save the time otherwise spent in going and coming. Most people do not have a really good day school at their doors, and the distance to be traversed may be considerable. This argument is strongest in the country, as the other was strongest for town dwellers.

When it is desired to try any innovation in

educational methods, it is almost inevitable that
it should first be tried in a boarding school, because it is unlikely that the parents who believe
in it will all live within one small area.   This
does not apply to infants, because they are not
yet wholly in the grip of the education authorities; consequently Madame Montessori and
Miss McMillan were able to try their experiment upon the very poor.   Within the recognized school years, on the contrary, only the
rich are allowed to try experiments with their
children's education.   Most of them, naturally,
prefer what is old and conventional; the few
who desire anything else are geographically
widely distributed, and do not anywhere suffice
to support a day school.   Such experiments as
Bedales are only possible for boarding schools.

The arguments on the other side are, however, very considerable.   In a school, many
aspects of life do not appear: it is an artificial
world, whose problems are not those of the
world at large.   A boy who is only at home
during the holidays, when everybody makes a
fuss over him, is likely to acquire far less knowledge of life than a boy who is at home every
morning and evening.   This is, at present, less
true of girls, because more is demanded of them
in many homes; but in proportion as their education is assimilated to that of boys, their home
life also will become similar, and their present

greater knowledge of domestic affairs will disappear. After fifteen or sixteen, it is good for
boys and girls to have a certain share in parental
occupations and anxieties—not too much, it is
true, since that would interfere with education,
but still some, lest they should fail to realize
that the old people have their own life, their
own interests, and their own importance. In
the school, only young people count, and it is
for them that everything is done. In holidays,
the atmosphere of home is apt to be dominated
by the young people. Consequently they tend
to become arrogant and hard, ignorant of the
problems of adult life, and quite aloof from
their parents.

This state of affairs is apt to have a bad effect
upon the affections of young people. Their
affection for their parents becomes atrophied,
and they never have to learn to adjust themselves to people whose tastes and pursuits are
different from their own. I think this tends
towards a certain selfish completeness, a feeling of one's own personality as something
exclusive. The family is the most natural corrective of this tendency, since it is a unit composed of people of different ages and sexes, with
different functions to perform; it is organic, in
a way which a collection of homogeneous individuals is not. Parents love their children
largely because they give so much trouble; if

parents give no trouble to their children, their children will not take them seriously. But the trouble they give must be legitimate: it must be only such as is necessary if they are to do their work and have any life of their own. Respect for the rights of others is one of the things young people ought to learn, and it is more easily learnt in the family than elsewhere. It is good for boys and girls to know that their father can be harassed by worries and their mother worn out by a multiplicity of details. And it is good that filial affection should remain alive during adolescence. A world without family affection tends to become harsh and mechanical, composed of individuals who try to domineer, but become cringing if they fail. I fear that these bad effects are to a certain extent produced by sending children to boarding schools, and I regard them as sufficiently serious to offset great advantages.

It is of course true, as modern psychologists insist, that the excessive influence of father or mother is a very harmful thing. But I do not believe it is likely to exist where children have gone to school from the age of two or three, as I have suggested that they should. Day school from an early age affords, to my mind, the right compromise between parental domination and parental insignificance. So far as concerns the set of considerations with which we have just been occupied, this seems clearly the best course, given a good home.

In the case of sensitive boys, there is a certain risk in leaving them to the exclusive society of other boys. Boys of about twelve are, for the most part, at a rather barbarous and insensitive stage. Quite recently, at a leading English school, there was a case of a boy suffering grave bodily injury for being sympathetic to the Labour Party. Boys who differ from the average in their opinions and tastes are likely to suffer seriously. Even at the most modern and progressive boarding schools in existence, pro-Boers had a bad time during the Boer war. Any boy who is fond of reading, or does not dislike his work, is pretty sure to be ill-treated. In France, the cleverest boys go to the *Ecole Normale Supérieure* and do not mix any longer with the average. This plan certainly has advantages. It prevents the intellectuals from having their nerve broken and becoming sycophants of the average Philistine, as happens to many of them in this country. It avoids the strain and misery which an unpopular boy must suffer. It makes it possible to give to clever boys the kind of teaching which suits them, which goes at a much more rapid pace than is possible for the less intelligent. On the other hand, it isolates the intellectuals from the rest of the community in later life, and makes them, perhaps, less able to understand the average man. In spite of this possible disadvantage, I think it on the whole better than the British upper-class practice of torturing all boys who have exceptional brains or exceptional moral qualities, unless they happen also to be good at games.[1]

However, the savagery of boys is not incurable, and is in fact much less than it was. "Tom Brown's School Days" gives a black picture, which would be exaggerated if applied to the public schools of our own day. It would be still less applicable to boys who had had the kind of early training which we considered in previous chapters. I think also that co-education—which is possible at a boarding school, as Bedales shows—is likely to have a civilizing effect upon boys. I am chary of admitting native differences between the sexes, but I think that girls are less prone than boys to punish oddity by serious physical cruelty. At present, however, there are very few boarding schools to which I should venture to send a boy if he were above the average in intelligence, morals, or sensitiveness, or if he were not conservative in politics and orthodox in theology. For such boys, I am convinced that the existing school system for the sons of rich parents is bad. And

[1] The arguments in favour of segregating the able children are well stated in O'Shea, Chap. XIV.

among such boys are included almost all who have any exceptional merit.

Of the above considerations, both for and against boarding schools, there are only two that are essential and unalterable, and these two are on opposite sides. On the one side there is the benefit of the country and air and space; on the other, the family affections and the education derived from knowledge of family responsibilities. In the case of parents who live in the country, there is a different argument in favour of boarding schools, namely, the improbability of a really good day school in their neighbourhood. I do not think it is possible, in view of these conflicting considerations, to arrive at any general conclusion. Where children are so strong and vigorous that considerations of health need not be taken very seriously, one argument for boarding schools fails. Where they are very devoted to their parents, one argument for day schools fails, since the holidays will suffice to keep family affection alive, and term time may just prevent it from becoming excessive. A sensitive child of exceptional ability had better not go to boarding school, and in extreme cases had better not go to school at all. Of course, a good school is better than a bad home, and a good home is better than a bad school. But where both are good, each case must be decided on its merits.

So far, I have written from the standpoint of a well-to-do parent, to whom individual choice is possible. When the matter is considered politically, from the point of view of the community, other considerations enter in. We have on the one hand the expense of boarding schools, on the other the simplification of the housing problem if children are away from home. I hold strongly that, apart from a few rare cases, every one ought to have a scholastic education up to the age of eighteen, and exclusively vocational training should only begin after that age. Although much might be urged both ways on our present topic, the financial consideration will, for a long time to come, decide the question, in the case of most wage-earners' sons and daughters, in favour of day schools. Since there is no clear ground for thinking this decision wrong, we may accept it, in spite of the fact that it is not made on educational grounds.

CHAPTER XVIII

THE UNIVERSITY

In previous chapters, we have considered the education in character and knowledge which, in a good social system, should be open to everybody, and should in fact be enjoyed by everybody, except for serious special reasons such as musical genius. (It would have been unfortunate if Mozart had been obliged to learn ordinary school subjects up to the age of eighteen.) But even in an ideal community there would, I think, be many people who would not go to the university. I am convinced that, at present, only a minority of the population can profit by a scholastic education prolonged to the age of twenty-one or twenty-two. Certainly the idle rich who at present infest the older universities very often derive no benefit from them, but merely contract habits of dissipation. We have therefore to ask on what principle we are to select those who should go to the university. At present, they are in the main those whose parents can afford to send them, though this principle of selection is being increasingly modified by the scholarship system. Obviously, the principle of selection ought to be educational, not financial. A boy or girl of eighteen, who has had a good school education, is capable of doing useful work. If he or she is to be exempted for a further period of three or four years, the community has a right to expect that the time will be profitably employed. But before deciding who is to go to the university, we must have some view as to the function of the university in the life of the community.

British universities have passed through three stages, of which, however, the second is not yet wholly displaced by the third. At first, they were training colleges for the clergy, to whom, in the Middle Ages, learning was almost wholly confined. Then, with the renaissance, the idea gained ground that every well-to-do person ought to be educated, though women were supposed to need less education than men. "The education of a gentleman" was given at the universities throughout the seventeenth, eighteenth and nineteenth centuries, and is still given at Oxford. For reasons which we considered in Chapter I, this ideal, which was formerly very useful, is now out-of-date; it depended upon aristocracy, and cannot flourish either in a democracy or in an industrial plutocracy. If there is to be an aristocracy, it had better be composed of educated gentlemen; but it is better still to have no aristocracy. I need not argue this question, since it was decided in England by the Reform Bill and the repeal of the Corn Laws, and in America by the War of Independence. It is true that we still have in England the forms of aristocracy, but the spirit is that of plutocracy, which is quite a different thing. Snobbery makes successful business men send their sons to Oxford to be turned into "gentlemen", but the result is to give them a distaste for business, which reduces their children again to comparative poverty and the need of earning a living. The "education of a gentleman" has therefore ceased to be an important part of the life of the nation, and may be ignored in considering the future.

The universities are thus reverting to a position more analogous to that which they occupied in the Middle Ages; they are becoming training schools for the professions. Barristers, clergymen and medical men have usually had a university education; so have the first division of the civil service. An increasing number of engineers and technical workers in various businesses are university men. As the world grows more complicated and industry becomes more scientific, an increasing number of experts are required, and in the main they are supplied by the universities. Old-fashioned people lament the intrusion of technical schools into the haunts of pure learning, but it continues none the less, because it is demanded by plutocrats who care nothing for "culture". It is they, much more than the insurgent democracy, who are the enemies of pure learning. "Useless" learning, like "art for art's sake", is an aristocratic, not a plutocratic, ideal; where it lingers, it is because the renaissance tradition is not yet dead. I regret the decay of this ideal profoundly; pure learning was one of the best things associated with aristocracy. But the evils of aristocracy were so great as easily to outweigh this merit. In any case, industrialism must kill aristocracy, whether we desire it or not. We may as well make up our minds, therefore, to save what we can by attaching it to new and more potent conceptions; so long as we cling to mere tradition, we shall be fighting a losing battle.

If pure learning is to survive as one of the purposes of universities, it will have to be brought into relation with the life of the community as a whole, not only with the refined delights of a few gentlemen of leisure. I regard disinterested learning as a matter of great importance, and I should wish to see its place in academic life increased, not diminished. Both in England and in America, the main force tending to its diminution has been the desire to get endowments from ignorant millionaires. The cure lies in the creation of an educated democracy, willing to spend public money on objects which our captains of industry are unable to appreciate. This is by no means impossible, but it demands a general raising of the intellectual level. It would be much facilitated if our learned men would more frequently emancipate themselves from the attitude of hangers-on of the rich, which they have inherited from a time when patrons were their natural source of livelihood. It is of course possible to confound learning with learned men. To take a purely imaginary example, a learned man may improve his financial position by teaching brewing instead of organic chemistry; he gains, but learning suffers. If the learned man had a more genuine love of learning, he would not be politically on the side of the brewer who endows a professorship of brewing. And if he were on the side of democracy, democracy would be more ready to see the value of his learning. For all these reasons, I should wish to see learned bodies dependent upon public money rather than upon the benefactions of rich men. This evil is greater in America than in England, but it exists in England, and may increase.

Leaving aside these political considerations, I

shall assume that universities exist for two purposes: on the one hand, to train men and women for certain professions; on the other hand, to pursue learning and research without regard to immediate utility. We shall therefore wish to see at the universities those who are going to practise these professions, and those who have that special kind of ability which will enable them to be valuable in learning and research. But this does not decide, by itself, how we are to select the men and women for the professions.

At present, it is very difficult to enter upon such a profession as law or medicine unless one's parents have a certain amount of money, since the training is expensive and earnings do not begin at once. The consequence is that the principle of selection is social and hereditary, not fitness for the work. Take medicine as illustrative. A community which wished to have its doctoring done efficiently would select for medical training those young people who showed most keenness and aptitude for the work. At present this principle is applied partially, to select among those who can afford the training; but it is quite probable that many of those who would make the best doctors are too poor to take the course. This involves a deplorable waste of talent. Let us take another example of a somewhat different kind. England is a very thickly populated country, which imports most of its food. From a number of points of view, but especially from that of safety in war, it would be a boon if more of our food were produced at home. Yet no measures are taken to see that our very limited area is efficiently cultivated. Farmers are selected mainly by heredity: as a rule, they are the sons of farmers. The others are men who have bought farms, which implies some capital but not necessarily any agricultural skill. It is known that Danish methods of agriculture are more productive than ours, but no steps are taken to cause our farmers to know about them. We ought to insist that every person allowed to cultivate more than a small holding should have a diploma in scientific agriculture, just as we insist on a motorist having a licence. The hereditary principle has been abandoned in government, but it lingers in many other departments of life. Wherever it exists, it promotes the inefficiency to which it formerly led in public affairs. We must replace it by two correlative rules: first, that no one shall be allowed to undertake important work without having acquired the necessary skill; secondly, that this skill shall be taught to the ablest of those who desire it, quite independently of their parents' means. It is obvious that these two rules would enormously increase efficiency.

University education should therefore be regarded as a privilege for special ability, and those who possess the skill but no money should be maintained at the public expense during their course. No one should be admitted unless he satisfies the tests of ability, and no one should be allowed to remain unless he satisfies the authorities that he is using his time to advantage. The idea of the university as a place of leisure where rich young men loaf for three or four years is dying, but, like Charles II, it is an unconscionable time about it.

When I say that a young man or woman at the university should not be allowed to be idle, I must hasten to add that the tests of work must not consist in a mechanical conformity to system. In the newer universities in England and America there is a regrettable tendency to insist upon attendance at innumerable lectures. The arguments in favour of individual work, which are allowed to be strong in the case of infants in a Montessori school, are very much stronger in the case of young people of twenty, particularly when, as we are assuming, they are keen and exceptionally able. When I was an undergraduate, my feeling, and that of most of my friends, was that lectures were a pure waste of time. No doubt we exaggerated, but not much. The real reason for lectures is that they are obvious work, and therefore business men are willing to pay for them. If university teachers adopted the best methods, business men would think them idle, and insist upon cutting down the staff. Oxford and Cambridge, because of their prestige, are to some extent able to apply the right methods; but the newer universities are unable to stand up against business men, and so are most American universities. The teacher should, at the beginning of the term, give a list of books to be read carefully, and a slight account of other books which some may like and others not. He should set papers, which can only be answered by noticing the important points in the books intelligently. He should see the pupils individually when they have done their papers. About once a week or once a fortnight, he should see such as care to come in the evening, and have desultory conversation about matters more or less connected with their work. All this is not very different from the practice at the older universities. If a pupil chooses to set himself a paper, different from that of the teacher but equally difficult, he shall be at liberty to do so. The industry of the pupils can be judged by their papers.

There is, however, one point of great importance. Every university teacher should be himself engaged in research, and should have sufficient leisure and energy to know what is being done in his subject in all countries. In university teaching, skill in pedagogy is no longer important; what is important is knowledge of one's subject and keenness about what is being done in it. This is impossible for a man who is overworked and nervously exhausted by teaching. His subject is likely to become distasteful to him, and his knowledge is almost sure to be confined to what he learnt in youth. Every university teacher ought to have a Sabbatical year (one in every seven), to be spent in foreign universities or in otherwise acquiring knowledge of what is being done abroad. This is common in America, but European countries have too much intellectual pride to admit that it is necessary. In this they are quite mistaken. The men who taught me mathematics at Cambridge were almost wholly untouched by the Continental mathematics of the previous twenty or thirty years; throughout my undergraduate time, I never heard the name of Weierstrass. It was only by subsequent travel that I came in contact with modern mathematics. This was no rare or exceptional circumstance. Of many universities at many periods similar things could be said.

There is in universities a certain opposition between those who care most for teaching and those who care most for research. This is almost entirely due to a wrong conception of teaching, and to the presence of a number of students whose industry and capacity are below the level which ought to be exacted as a condition of residence. The idea of the old-fashioned schoolmaster persists to some extent at universities. There is a desire to have a good moral effect on students, and a wish to drill them in old-fashioned worthless information, largely known to be false but supposed to be morally elevating. Students ought not to be exhorted to work, but they should not be allowed to remain if they are found to be wasting their time, whether from idleness or from lack of ability. The only morality which can be profitably exacted is that of work; the rest belongs to earlier years. And the morality of work should be exacted by sending away those who do not possess it, since evidently they had better be otherwise employed. A teacher should not be expected to work long hours at teaching, and should have abundant leisure for research; but he should be expected to employ this leisure wisely.

Research is at least as important as education, when we are considering the functions of universities in the life of mankind. New knowledge is the chief cause of progress, and without it the world would soon become stationary. It could continue, for a time, to improve by the diffusion and wider use of existing knowledge, but this process, by itself, could not last long. And even the pursuit of knowledge, if it is utilitarian, is not self-sustaining. Utilitarian knowledge needs to be fructified by disinterested investigation, which has no motive beyond the desire to understand the world better. All the great advances are at first purely theoretical, and are only afterwards found to be capable of practical applications. And even if some splendid theory never has any practical use, it remains of value on its own account; for the understanding of the world is one of the ultimate goods. If science and organization had succeeded in satisfying the needs of the body and in abolishing cruelty and war, the pursuit of knowledge and beauty would remain to exercise our love of strenuous creation. I should not wish the poet, the painter, the composer or the mathematician to be preoccupied with some remote effect of his activities in the world of practice. He should be occupied, rather, in the pursuit of a vision, in capturing and giving permanence to something which he has first seen dimly for a moment, which he has loved with such ardour that the joys of this world have grown pale by comparison. All great art and all great science springs from the passionate desire to embody what was at first an unsubstantial phantom, a beckoning beauty luring men away from safety and ease to a glorious torment. The men in whom this passion exists must not be fettered by the shackles of a utilitarian philosophy, for to their ardour we owe all that makes man great.

CHAPTER XIX

AT the end of our journey, let us look back over the road, to obtain a bird's-eye view of the country we have traversed.

Knowledge wielded by love is what the educator needs and what his pupils should acquire. In earlier years, love towards the pupils is the most important kind; in later years, love of the knowledge imparted becomes increasingly necessary. The important knowledge at first is knowledge of physiology, hygiene, and psychology, of which the last more especially concerns the teacher. The instincts and reflexes with which a child is born can be developed by the environment into the most diverse habits, and therefore into the most diverse characters. Most of this happens in very early childhood; consequently it is at this period that we can most hopefully attempt to form character. Those who like existing evils are fond of asserting that human nature cannot be changed. If they mean that it cannot be changed after six years old, there is a measure of truth in what they say. If they mean that nothing can be done to alter the instincts and reflexes with which an infant is born, they are again more or less in the right, though of course eugenics could, and perhaps will, produce remarkable results even here. But if they mean, as they usually do, that there is no way of producing an adult population whose behaviour will be radically different from that of existing populations, they are flying in the face of all modern psychology. Given two infants with the same character at birth, different early environments may turn them into adults with totally different dispositions. It is the business of early education to train the instincts so that they may produce a harmonious character, constructive rather than destructive, affectionate rather than sullen, courageous, frank, and intelligent. All this can be done with a great majority of children; it is actually being done where children are rightly treated. If existing knowledge were used and tested methods applied, we could, in a generation, produce a population almost wholly free from disease, malevolence, and stupidity. We do not do so, because we prefer oppression and war.

The crude material of instinct is, in most respects, equally capable of leading to desirable and to undesirable actions. In the past, men did not understand the training of instinct, and therefore were compelled to resort to repression.   Punishment and fear were the great incentives to what was called virtue.   We now know that repression is a bad method, both because it is never really successful, and because it produces mental disorders.   The training of instincts is a totally different method, involving a totally different technique.   Habits and skill make, as it were, a channel for instinct, leading it to flow one way or another according to the direction of the channel.   By creating the right habits and the right skill, we cause the child's instincts themselves to prompt desirable actions. There is no sense of strain, because there is no need to resist temptation.   There is no thwarting, and the child has a sense of unfettered spontaneity.   I do not mean these statements to be taken in an absolute sense; there will always be unforeseen contingencies in which older methods may become necessary.   But the more the science of child psychology is perfected, and the more experience we acquire in nursery-schools, the more perfectly the new methods can be applied.

I have tried to bring before the reader the wonderful possibilities which are now open to us.   Think what it would mean: health, freedom, happiness, kindness, intelligence, all nearly universal.   In one generation, if we chose, we could bring the millennium.

But none of this can come about without love.

The knowledge exists; lack of love prevents it from being applied. Sometimes the lack of love towards children brings me near to despair —for example, when I find almost all our recognized moral leaders unwilling that anything should be done to prevent the birth of children with venereal disease. Nevertheless, there is a gradual liberation of love of children, which surely is one of our natural impulses. Ages of fierceness have overlaid what is naturally kindly in the dispositions of ordinary men and women. It is only lately that many Christians have ceased to teach the damnation of unbaptized infants. Nationalism is another doctrine which dries up the springs of humanity; during the war, we caused almost all German children to suffer from rickets. We must let loose our natural kindliness; if a doctrine demands that we should inflict misery upon children, let us reject it, however dear it may be to us. In almost all cases, the psychological source of cruel doctrines is fear; that is one reason why I have laid so much stress upon the elimination of fear in childhood. Let us root out the fears that lurk in the dark places of our own minds. The possibilities of a happy world that are opened up by modern education make it well worth while to run some personal risk, even if the risk were more real than it is.

When we have created young people freed

from fear and inhibitions and rebellious or
thwarted instincts, we shall be able to open to
them the world of knowledge, freely and completely, without dark hidden corners; and if
instruction is wisely given, it will be a joy
rather than a task to those who receive it.   It is
not important to increase the amount of what is
learnt above that now usually taught to the
children of the professional classes.   What is
important is the spirit of adventure and liberty,
the sense of setting out upon a voyage of discovery.   If formal education is given in this
spirit, all the more intelligent pupils will supplement it by their own efforts, for which every
opportunity should be provided.   Knowledge
is the liberator from the empire of natural
forces and destructive passions; without knowledge, the world of our hopes cannot be built.
A generation educated in fearless freedom will
have wider and bolder hopes than are possible
to us, who still have to struggle with the super-
stitious fears that lie in wait for us below the
level of consciousness.   Not we, but the free
men and women whom we shall create, must see
the new world, first in their hopes, and then
at last in the full splendour of reality.

The way is clear.   Do we love our children
enough to take it?   Or shall we let them suffer
as we have suffered?   Shall we let them be
twisted and stunted and terrified in youth, to be

killed afterwards in futile wars which their intelligence was too cowed to prevent? A thousand ancient fears obstruct the road to happiness and freedom. But love can conquer fear, and if we love our children nothing can make us withhold the great gift which it is in our power to bestow.

THE END